Anatomy of
Error

Also by Henry Brandon

AS WE ARE

CONVERSATIONS WITH HENRY BRANDON

IN THE RED

ANATOMY OF ERROR

The Inside Story of the Asian
War on the Potomac, 1954–1969

HENRY BRANDON

Gambit
INCORPORATED
Boston

1969

First Printing

© Copyright 1969 by Times Newspapers Ltd.
Published in Great Britain by André Deutsch Limited
All rights reserved including the right to reproduce this book
    or parts thereof in any form
Library of Congress Catalog Card Number: 75-95232
Printed in the United States of America

To

Richard and Bert

Foreword

The Editor-in-Chief of The Times Newspapers, Denis Hamilton, the Editor of the *Sunday Times*, Harold Evans, and the Editorial Page Editor of the *Washington Post*, Philip L. Geyelin, encouraged me to embark on this undertaking. Admittedly it was a highly ambitious one, with the ink of many of the decisions scarcely dry and only limited time at my disposal. For the deeper I dug into the subject, the more I realized how bottomless the well is, how deceptive memories, especially when charged with emotion, can be. But editors and book publishers insist on deadlines. Without the thoughtful assistance and editorial expertise of Oscar Turnill, an Assistant Editor of the *Sunday Times*, and the diligence and unfailing cheerfulness of my personal assistant, Nora Leake, who typed the entire manuscript, this long-distance sprint into history would have been a lonely and unbearable race. I also owe an enormous amount of gratitude to all those who allowed me to rummage in their memories and on whose collective testimony this book is based. For obvious reasons most of them wanted to remain anonymous; but without their cooperation this book would have been impossible. About half the material contained in this book appeared in a series of three articles in the London *Sunday Times* on April 13, 20, and 27, 1969, under the title, "The Unwinnable War."

CONTENTS

Anatomy of
Error

Prologue:
The War That Went Wrong

In the most unexpected way, the war in Vietnam has had a devastating effect on Americans. This faraway war in the defense of people they hardly know, even today, has created deep chasms among adults and helped to trigger a rebellion among the young. It has destroyed many well-established assumptions. It has led to the abdication of the American President and the electoral defeat of his party, and has cruelly scarred the United States' reputation in the world.

The war has undermined Americans' confidence in the judgment of their leaders, in their institutions, their military Establishment, their foreign policy. It has inflamed the young to the extent that they have begun to resist military service as perhaps never before in American history. It has engendered an anti-militarist feeling that—while it has its healthy aspects—has made the U.S. Government and its allies a little uneasy as to what extent, in such circumstances, it is possible to count on the American will to help support the President in shouldering his worldwide responsibilities.

Considering all these grave consequences, I felt tempted to find out how the United States could have allowed herself to be dragged into so catastrophic an adventure. What were the missed chances and miscalculations? Whose influences were responsible for so much mishap? How did it happen that men of great experience, high intelligence, and essentially peaceful intentions became embroiled in this unheroic, unwinnable war? Did the fault lie in the very early moves of President Truman and President Eisenhower, or are President Kennedy's decisions to blame? Or was it all President Johnson's fault? And what do those who helped to shape the fatal course themselves now think of their parts in this abrasive history?

I interviewed virtually all the principal actors, many of the minor ones, even some of the stagehands, in order to piece this history together. Some among them have confided to me that they would not trust themselves to write such a history, even with all the secret documentation at their disposal: they felt they still could not take a sufficiently detached view. Many disagree about the cause and purpose of the war, about its conduct, and about decisions of policy and how they were made. They also tend to disagree about the lessons that should be drawn from this bitter experience. Many of the men responsible for critical decisions are still reluctant to discuss their dilemmas or their mistakes. Some are as convinced as ever that they acted rightly; others are now plagued by doubt and even conscience.

In many ways these men reflect the deep and continuing conflicts that the war has aroused in all Americans.

These contradictions, of course, made it often very difficult to get to the truth; and it may be objected, therefore, that the time has not yet come for proper assessment. After all, the larger wounds, even if they are several years old, are still raw, still hurting. Might it not be too difficult to apply the necessary perspective at this stage, and unwise to rely on individual recollection? But in this respect I drew some comfort from the reactions to Robert Kennedy's short, intimate history of the Cuban missile crisis. He had, after all, as thorough a knowledge as anyone of what happened then. Robert McNamara, one of those present at all the important meetings, is convinced that Robert Kennedy's tale is accurate. But when I discussed his book recently with Dean Rusk, the former Secretary of State declared flatly that it was badly distorted history; he felt so strongly about it, he said, that he would write his own version. Such disagreements at high levels gave me courage to persist in what some will call my precipitateness in attempting this account of the war.

What was particularly helpful to me in dealing with this subject was the fact that I have reported events from Washington ever since American interest in Vietnam, and the war, began. I also spent time in Indochina (as it was then called) with the French in the early fifties, and later with the American forces. In this book I have ignored the war on the ground (apart from necessary observance of the build-up of the American commitment) and concentrated on what I believe to be the crucial military and political decisions—and these, of course, were almost all taken in Washington.

Once it was decided not to carry the war into North Vietnam, or not to deny the enemy his sanctuaries in Laos or Cambodia, I maintain that it became impossible to win a decisive victory. This does not mean that I do not fully agree with the decision against widening the war; this could have meant not only Chinese intervention, as in Korea, and further aggravation of the Kremlin's dilemma about how far to commit Soviet resources, but also a commitment of American forces to a degree that would have seriously distorted the distribution of American power throughout the world. The assassin's bullets in Sarajevo led to a world war of proportions nobody had originally contemplated, and the attempt to destroy North Vietnam could have had the same effect.

Nor do I subscribe to the idea that the war was lost at home because American public opinion turned against it. It is closer to the truth to say that the U.S. failed militarily because the American forces did not train and equip the South Vietnamese adequately until 1967-68, but believed they could win the war by themselves. Politically, the U.S. failed because President Johnson and his military leaders thought they could ignore public opinion. On my return from Vietnam in

4

November, 1967, it was quite obvious that public opposition to the war was rising rapidly in the U.S. The President not only underrated the power of public opinion, he rode roughshod over it; and he tended to place too much trust in the judgment of the military, who constantly held out the promise, specter though it might be, of military victory. In Vietnam, the military refused to include in their calculations the state of American public opinion. They insisted to me in Saigon that they did not need to do so; this, they said, was President Johnson's responsibility. And of course it was an informed public opinion, informed not only because of the absence of censorship but also because of the immediacy of "living color" television reporting.

Considering the public groundswell against the war and the stalemated military situation on the ground, I was then convinced that the war could not be won, and that the U.S. could only hold out long enough for a compromise settlement if it winched down the cost in men and materiel. To cool American opinion was, at that stage, much more important than trying to pursue the chimera of military victory, especially in a war that did not lend itself to the heroic or the spectacular, but looked to Americans increasingly like that proverbial "rathole."

There was a clear need to set a limit somehow to the investment the U.S. was willing to risk. But this was never done; on the contrary, the impression was created that there was no limit to the investment. The more

5

Americans came to feel that the war was not an essential American interest, the more those in charge tried to prove the opposite. But they could not arrest the strong feeling that the U.S. did not need Vietnam as a military base and that economically it was of no importance to America. Furthermore, the case of aggression was not as clear as it had been in Korea. The war remained basically an insurgency, helped and abetted and exploited by North Vietnam. It is true that in the end North Vietnamese units represented the bulk of the enemy forces, but without the insurgency in the South, Hanoi would have found it very difficult, if not impossible, to fight this war.

Strategically, perhaps there was a U.S. interest, since it had been basic American foreign policy to contain Communism and prevent its expansion. Such a policy remained viable only as long as it did not involve the U.S. in exorbitant risks and costs. I doubt whether Mr. Truman, Mr. Eisenhower, Mr. Kennedy, or even Mr. Johnson would have pursued the U.S. commitment in Vietnam had they known how deeply the United States would become involved and at what cost. Not even the marginal strategic national interest would have been enough.

Instead of insisting on its original aim—an independent, non-Communist South Vietnam—the U.S. has now been forced to retreat to letting the South Vietnamese decide their own ultimate fate in a contest between Communists and non-Communists. The U.S. had no choice, because, as that outstanding reporter-analyst Stewart Alsop put it, "The American people lost stomach for the war in Vietnam." He added: "People who have lost stomach for a war in the end generally lose the war. If that happens, it will be interesting, if perhaps a bit frightening, to see how the American people react to their first lost war."

As well as this severe indigestion in the American "stomach," the war in Vietnam has provoked a bitter and divisive debate about the rights and wrongs of American foreign policy. There is basically no harm, perhaps a lot of good, in such a debate, but it is occurring under circumstances and in a mood that has both weakened the powers of the President of the United States and given serious momentum to an isolationist trend—the very opposite of what the advocates of the war in Vietnam intended.

I

Truman to Kennedy:
Half-Measures

On April 2, 1954, I sat in Mr. John Foster Dulles's ante-room at the State Department, waiting to see him. That week, and even earlier, the signs had begun to accumulate that the United States was preparing to go into what was then called the Indochina War on the side of the hard-pressed French, who were fighting that decisive, final battle of Dien Bien Phu. Mr. Dulles himself, on the previous Monday, had made a speech advocating "direct action," but had left commentators to assume that he was preparing for direct military action. I had asked for my appointment more than a week earlier; suddenly, that Friday morning, his secretary had telephoned to ask if I could come to see him immediately, at noon.

Mr. Dulles was his usual calm self, except that behind his gold-rimmed glasses his eyes twitched a little more nervously than usual. After a few preliminaries I asked the key question: had he meant to herald America's entry into the Indochina War? Mr. Dulles leaned forward, then tipped his chair back. After a long pause he spoke, emphasizing every word: "I can tell you that American aircraft carriers are at this moment steaming into the Gulf of Tonkin, ready to strike."

He seemed to take some pleasure in dropping this bombshell into my journalistic lap. But when I asked him to clarify—had the U.S. in fact decided to intervene?—he hesitated for a moment, then said slowly, "Not yet." He went on to explain that the U.S. Government was convinced that it could not afford to let Indochina go Communist. He favored intervention, but President Eisenhower had made such action dependent on Britain's deciding to go in, and Prime Minister Anthony Eden was stubbornly opposed to the idea.

I knew, as Mr. Dulles must have known, that the British Cabinet was to meet in two days' time, on Sunday; a lot depended on that meeting, and I was certain, as I sat down to write my weekly dispatch to the *Sunday Times* (in which I could not quote from the interview), that in indicating such sensational developments Mr. Dulles was hoping to use one more avenue to influence the climate of opinion in London, hoping to enlist support for a carrier-based air strike to assist the beleaguered French garrison at Dien Bien Phu.

Intervention was his idea and that of Admiral Radford, then Chairman of the Joint Chiefs of Staff, and was favored by Vice-President Richard M. Nixon.

In the end, President Eisenhower's refusal to intervene without the British, and the rapid deterioration of the French position at Dien Bien Phu, put an end to the plan. Ironically, those who agreed with the President in opposing the plan and who insisted on enlisting allied support included Senator Lyndon B. Johnson.

America's involvement in Vietnam actually began when President Franklin D. Roosevelt, influenced by Prime Minister Winston Churchill, agreed to allow the French government to reassert control in Indochina. The seed for the Viet Minh struggle for national independence was then sown, and it grew as the French attempted to re-establish themselves in their former colonies. In a deceptively diplomatic way, as more and more French soldiers were sent to fight and die in Indochina, the U.S. allowed her commitment to take root.

President Truman was the first to pledge American economic and military aid to permit Indochina "to pursue peaceful and democratic development"; and it was his Secretary of State, Dean Acheson, who, on February 2, 1950, first identified their ultimate opponent. Russia's recognition of Ho Chi Minh's Communist movement, he said then, "reveals Ho in his true colors as the mortal enemy of native independence in Indochina." Acheson's overriding concern, however, was in fact less the Vietnamese people and their future than the desire to preserve close Franco-American relations and promote European unification. The limited American interest in the area was reflected by the fact that in 1950 the U.S. had a combined total of eight diplomatic representatives in Vietnam, Laos, and Cambodia.

Six months after my meeting with Mr. Dulles, President Eisenhower elaborated the Truman theme of aid, promising "to assist the government of Vietnam in maintaining a strong, viable state, capable of resisting attempted subversion or aggression through military means."

Still there was no commitment, though gradually an American ideological interest was being staked out. It was inspired by the Truman doctrine that aggressive Communism (in this case Chinese Communism) had to be stopped, and the fear that a Communist takeover would promote a strong, hostile Asia. It was checked by a certain ambivalence—founded in the innate American distaste for appearing to help an old colonial power maintain its influence—though that disappeared once the French withdrew.

Gradually a certain state of mind was created in the United States about the importance of Indochina. Certain premises were established, though they were not carefully thought through, and certain dogmas began to develop. As aid to Saigon increased, and especially military aid, so American statesmen emphasized their country's stake in the area. And as the need to intensify the aid grew, so did the emphasis, and gradually it became a part of American foreign policy. American prestige became involved.

Republicans like to point to Truman's pledges of aid as the beginning of the American commitment; President Johnson always referred to the Eisenhower letter

of 1954 as the starting point. But still there was no commitment, as President Johnson was later to claim there
was (the SEATO commitment was not invoked by the
United States until April, 1964); and there was a condition. The American effort, in President Eisenhower's
words, was based on "performance" by the Saigon Government in "undertaking needed reforms."

In 1954 the Geneva Conference produced accords on
the cessation of hostilities that enabled France to withdraw gracefully. It also created what was meant to be
a provisional division between what have since become
known as North and South Vietnam. Since the North
was Ho's, America's concern was thus with the non-
Communist South, and the man who emerged to head
the government there was Ngo Dinh Diem. It was when
President Eisenhower decided to find out, in the spring
of 1955, whether or not he should back Diem that a certain trend set in.

Eisenhower sent General "Lightning Joe" Collins to
Saigon as a detached observer. Whatever recommendation he brought back, the President promised, would
get the most serious consideration. Collins returned
firmly convinced that America should not prop up
Diem, but instead support the French preference for
someone who could bridge the differences between the
South and the North. Few credited General Collins with
much political acumen, and many shrugged off his report. It was the subject of a tempestuous meeting pre-
sided over by John Foster Dulles, whose views were

backed by the Central Intelligence Agency (which in turn was primarily influenced by Colonel Edward G. Lansdale, a man whose passion for and commitment to the South Vietnamese cause likened him to Lawrence of Arabia; Lansdale is also said to have inspired Graham Greene's *Quiet American*). Dulles and the CIA won the day. The United States pinned its flag to President Diem as the savior of Vietnam from Communism, and the hope was that the South Vietnamese Army, whose training the U.S. had taken over, would be able to keep the situation under control.

By then the French were already convinced, as they had been when I first went to Vietnam in 1953, that the war was lost, and that the last chance to retrieve it had been missed around 1950.

True, Diem lasted for eight years after General Collins wanted him to be abandoned. But in those eight years divisions in Vietnam deepened until they became unbridgeable. By the time President Kennedy took over from Eisenhower in January, 1961, Vietnam had become not only a foreign but also a domestic American problem.

From the record of President Eisenhower's briefing of his successor, it is evident that he focused almost entirely on the dangerous situation in Laos, Vietnam's neighbor to the west. Mr. Eisenhower advised making every effort to obtain a political solution; but, he said, if this proved fruitless he would recommend military intervention, if possible under the SEATO agreement.

This treaty, by establishing an American commitment for future intervention in Asia, was John Foster Dulles's way of extricating himself from political accusations that he had failed to save the French from defeat. President Eisenhower also went as far as suggesting to President Kennedy that if the United States failed to persuade her allies to support military intervention in Laos, that country was sufficiently important for America to "go it alone." (This was curiously in contrast to Eisenhower's attitude a few months earlier, when at a National Security Council meeting he had called the Joint Chiefs of Staff "stupid" for proposing to send two American divisions to Laos.)

Soon after his inauguration President Kennedy asked the Joint Chiefs of Staff for an estimate of what intervention in Laos would involve. The first estimate was about 45,000 men, or one division. But when Kennedy questioned whether one division would really be enough, the Joint Chiefs' estimate shot up as high as 300,000 men; they added that this presupposed that the United States, in order to succeed, would be ready to use, if necessary, all weapons in its arsenal, which meant nuclear weapons.

When Kennedy discussed the Laotian situation with Prime Minister Harold Macmillan at their first meeting in Florida, he failed to enlist his support, and gradually, the more he examined the situation, the more he became convinced that he did not want to get bogged down in Laos, that, on the contrary, disengagement was the wiser alternative. So he asked Ambassador Averell Harriman, one of the greatest American statesmen-diplomats, who had learned under at least three Presidents how to keep a secret, to negotiate this disengagement from Laos. It was characteristic of Kennedy's way of making up his mind privately about doing something that he knew would be unpopular both inside his administration and among the public.

With his secret instructions Harriman received the President's assurance that he would give him full support in this delicate operation. Harriman never hesitated to accept such difficult and confidential assignments; he had accomplished almost everything that a statesman-diplomat might aspire to; and at that stage of his career he was, as he once put it to President Johnson, "expendable." It proved to be a long and trying assignment, made more difficult and exasperating by the fact that war was always at the negotiators' doorstep.

At one point the military situation had become so serious that it looked as if the Pathet Lao, the Communist forces, would terrify General Phoumi's loyalist army into defeat. To counter this threat, Kennedy was pressed, especially by Michael Forrestal (then on the staff of McGeorge Bundy, the President's adviser on Security Affairs), to send a battalion of marines to Thailand just opposite the Laotian border and units of the Seventh Fleet ostentatiously into the Gulf of Tonkin, to signal American readiness to intervene if necessary. Kennedy agreed to both reluctantly, but when he ordered the dispatch of the marine battalion he called in Forrestal and asked him whether he was now satisfied. He added, "And now tell me how we get them out if they are attacked." Forrestal then drafted a memorandum on how they should be withdrawn.

The situation in Vietnam at that time did not seem as urgent as that in Laos. But on May 5, 1961, Kennedy announced that he was sending Vice-President Lyndon B. Johnson on a fact-finding mission to Asia, and when asked at a press conference whether he would be prepared to send troops into South Vietnam, he replied that the matter of assisting that country in maintaining its independence was still under consideration.

It was, in fact, reviewed by a task force set up by Kennedy and headed by Roswell Gilpatrick, Deputy Secretary of Defense, and Edward Lansdale of the CIA. They came up with very limited recommendations. The emphasis was on an increase in economic and military aid, certain political actions, and so on, but nobody advocated any drastic remedies. Not even Secretary of State Dean Rusk felt strongly in those days about the American stake in Vietnam; he even warned, in a memorandum, against becoming too deeply involved, arguing that once the U.S. was committed it would be difficult to get out.

Not until October of that year, when he sent two of his advisers, General Maxwell Taylor and Walt W. Rostow, to South Vietnam, did Kennedy become more deeply involved. Diem had asked for enough money and equipment to increase his own armed forces by 100,000 men to fight local insurgents. Kennedy showed Diem's letter to General Taylor, and asked for his comments and how to reply "to avoid further deterioration of the situation in South Vietnam and to eventually contain and eliminate the threat to its independence." What sticks in Taylor's mind now is that the President did *not* ask him whether the U.S. should intervene or pull out altogether.

After ten days in Vietnam, Taylor and Rostow wrote their report and submitted it to Kennedy on November 3. It was very carefully phrased, and its basic theme was how best to save a bad situation. Some would call it a prescient document, some an ominous one, for it set a direction—it recommended the first important escalation of the American involvement in Vietnam.

They advised that an emergency program should be implemented without delay; that in their judgment the problem was "serious" but by no means "hopeless"; and that if American resources were properly applied there were "high odds for ultimate success." Many in the Administration interpreted this as meaning that things would get worse if the U.S. did not enter the war, but that with time military support would turn events to the United States' advantage.

The recommendations were for a partnership approach with the South Vietnamese Government. This meant active participation of American advisers in government administration, military planning, intelligence

(Taylor was struck by the unreliability of the available data), and in flood relief for the Mekong Delta, which was almost totally under water. Taylor admits that he was overly impressed by this disaster situation. One recommendation, never fulfilled, was for investigators to discover what went on in the countryside; Taylor felt they depended too much on what Diem told them. But Diem was reluctant to let Americans into the provinces, and in any case until 1964 there were too few American Vietnamese experts to undertake such missions—a deficiency that many blame in retrospect for the mistakes made.

The objectives of the military recommendations were to retrain the South Vietnamese Army into a mobile instead of a static force, and to develop its offensive capability by bringing in helicopters and light aircraft. Americans would help in air reconnaissance and aerial photography, in which the South Vietnamese were not trained, and American naval craft would survey and stop coastal shipping (though the stopping of enemy ships would be left to Vietnamese boats only).

Added to this, there would be more economic aid and the sending of a small task force, mostly of engineers, to help in flood relief. This task force would be accompanied by an unstated but limited number of troops to protect them and stay as long as the flood situation persisted.

The light aircraft would be flown by Vietnamese, with American copilots. There was no recommendation to bomb the North (as has been variously suggested), though it was pointed out that the time might come when the U.S. would have to consider whether it could continue to allow the North Vietnamese a sanctuary.

The troops provided the most heated debate in the Administration, but, as it turned out, the floods soon subsided, and no organized units were sent. In that event Kennedy adopted only part of the prescription. But he did permit American military advisers to go into battle with Vietnamese troops, a careful and deliberate decision, and he allowed American pilots to fly for the South Vietnamese.

There were two reasons why he did so. One combined the memory of his Cuban blunder at the Bay of Pigs with his decision to seek a neutralist solution in Laos: he had to make a strong stand against Communism somewhere. The other was his fascination with the idea of preparing an American guerrilla force to fight against Communist "wars of liberation." The idea had been promoted by General Taylor and Roger Hilsman, a West Point graduate who had become director of the State Department Bureau of Intelligence and Research; it also appealed to Robert Kennedy.

Vietnam was to become the testing ground for this idea. It was part of the search for ways to exalt the role of the individual, the heroic man, in a world made too dangerous by the threat of nuclear war. It won expression in the creation both of the Peace Corps and of the Green Berets, the jungle-soldier equivalent of Britain's

World War Two Commandos (except that they were trained only for jungle warfare).

So, in 1961, Kennedy took himself in deeper. That year he increased the number of military advisers in Vietnam to 3,000 (when this number passed 600 the U.S. had technically breached the Geneva accords, but Kennedy and his advisers took the loose view that this violation was justified by Communist aggression in South Vietnam). In the next two years the number increased to 17,000.

In 1962 President Kennedy continued to receive conflicting advice. Robert McNamara, Secretary of Defense, reassured him that "every quantitative measurement we have shows we are winning the war." He also received, on April 4, a memorandum from his then Ambassador to India, John Kenneth Galbraith, which recommended the following guidelines for his policy in Vietnam:

1. We should resist all steps which commit American troops to combat action and impress upon all concerned the importance of keeping American forces out of actual combat commitment.
2. We should disassociate ourselves from action, however necessary, which seems to be directed at the villagers, such as the new concentration program. If the action is one that is peculiarly identified with Americans, such as defoliation, it should not be undertaken in the absence of most compelling reasons. Americans in their various roles should be as invisible as the situation permits.

21

The considerations which influenced Galbraith's thinking on Vietnam and on which he based his recommendations were these:

1. We have a growing military commitment. This could expand step by step into a major, long, drawn-out, indecisive military involvement.
2. We are backing a weak and, on the record, ineffectual government and a leader who as a politician may be beyond the point of no return.
3. There is a consequent danger that we shall replace the French as the colonial force in the area and bleed as the French did.
4. The political effects of some of the measures which pacification requires, or is believed to require, including the concentration of population, relocation of villages, and the burning of old villages, may be damaging to those, and especially Westerners, associated with it.
5. We fear that at some point in the involvement there will be a major political outburst about the new Korea and the new war into which the Democrats, as so often before, have precipitated us.
6. It seems at least possible that the Soviets are not particularly desirous of trouble in this part of the world and our military reaction with the need to fall back on Chinese protection may be causing concern in Hanoi.

But it was not until March, 1963, that Kennedy really focused on Vietnam. That spring many still thought that the U.S. was on the way to gaining control of the guerrilla war, though reports of infiltration from North Vietnam began to cause uneasiness. In October, Kennedy was encouraged when Mr. McNamara and

General Taylor, who had become Chairman of the Joint Chiefs of Staff, returned from Vietnam to announce that "the major part of the U.S. military task can be completed by the end of 1965."

In retrospect, Robert McNamara says: "We were told that we were making progress in South Vietnam, but we were not thinking about what the North Vietnamese were doing to offset these gains. Nor did we realize how weak Diem really was. We should have stopped in 1963, for there is a time limit to an advisory role; it did not help to improve the situation enough."

But at the same time a basic disagreement had set in among members of the U.S. Government over what the struggle was about, whether it was primarily a military problem, and whether a stable and viable South Vietnam would best be secured by the defeat of the guerrillas or by the American-imposed aid machine. The military saw it as a war to be won. General Earle G. Wheeler, who had suceeded Taylor as Chairman of the Joint Chiefs of Staff, discussed the war, saying, "It is fashionable in some quarters to say that the problems in Southeast Asia are primarily political and economic rather than military. I do not agree. The essence of the problem in Vietnam is military." For the Pentagon, therefore, it was best to cling to Diem, for he was the man actually in office.

For those who saw it as a political problem, however, hope of success lay primarily in the strategic hamlet scheme and the pacification program. Some compared the Vietnamese situation to that of Greece and its Communist guerrillas after World War Two. Some thought that the methods the British had used in Malaya could be applied in Vietnam. But such premises led only to false analogies; and partly because of that, and partly because the lessons were ineptly applied anyway, they led merely to failure.

The notion that the war was a political problem dominated in 1961 and 1962, but in September, 1963, President Kennedy, angry after the Buddhist revolt in South Vietnam that May, declared: "I don't think the war can be won unless the people support the effort, and in my opinion, in the last two months the government has gotten out of touch with the people." (Sir Robert K. G. Thompson, who made a name for himself in the Malayan war as a guerrilla expert and acted as adviser to the Americans, underlined that where a guerrilla force enjoys support from the people, whether willing or forced, it can never be defeated by military means.)

When Diem and Nhu, his brother-in-law and his Rasputin, who controlled both the police and the intelligence service, resisted American demands for political reforms, U.S. economic aid (including such commodities as condensed milk) was quietly cut off. The feeling in the National Security Council was that the U.S. should not abandon Vietnam, but that it could not continue aid under the prevailing conditions. As the internal political situation of South Vietnam deteriorated, the question was asked whether the U.S. should engage its own troops or whether it should withdraw entirely. The latter part of the question was raised by Robert Kennedy at the time.

In Saigon, meanwhile, the Vietnamese generals, themselves fiercely impatient with Diem and Nhu, were sharpening their knives. Ambassador Henry Cabot Lodge in Saigon and the so-called Harriman group in the State Department had both concluded that Diem's government had ceased to be viable.

A notorious cable was sent to Lodge—it was drafted by Harriman, George Ball, Michael Forrestal, and Roger Hilsman—proposing that a virtual ultimatum be given to Diem to rid himself of his brother-in-law, who had led the bloody attacks against the Buddhist pagodas. If Diem refused to unload Nhu, it was to be made clear to him that his regime could not be preserved. Kennedy was angry with Forrestal and Hilsman, not because he disagreed with the cable but because it had not been properly cleared and half the U.S. Government disagreed with it. Nevertheless, by early September, 1963, the President supported those who favored cutting off payments to the special forces Nhu used as his bodyguard, and cutting off the commodity program as well.

To the poised, plotting generals of South Vietnam this meant that the United States had lost faith in its chosen instrument. They first asked for direct support, but received a negative answer. In November the generals took matters into their own hands, and ousted and killed Diem. The Americans were ill-informed about what was afoot (the U.S. Admiral Felt overstayed his time during an interview with Diem and thus almost came in danger of being killed with him), but were acquiescent in the result, though they had not wanted Diem's death. Yet the removal of Diem solved nothing for them; it led only to the enlargement of the U.S. commitment. And within three weeks, President Kennedy himself died in Dallas.

Whether, despite his seemingly deepening commitment, Kennedy would have tried to extricate himself from the war is impossible to determine. The evidence is inconclusive, but both he and his brother had begun to question in discussion with some of their aides the fundamental assumptions of United States involvement. Robert Kennedy (according to Roger Hilsman's book *To Move a Nation*) raised the question whether it was possible for the U.S. to be helpful to a country whose political structure was so unformed.

What troubled him was that a group of irresponsible politicians in Saigon had such a hold on American power and prestige, far greater than was commensurate with the American commitment. This concern was later shared by President Johnson to the extent that he came close to desperation when coups constantly seemed to threaten the Saigon Government; but he did not question the commitment as the Kennedys did in the closing months of their Administration. Unconsciously the U.S.

had set up a client government; America did all the giving, Saigon, all the taking.

For all his frankness and directness in private conversation, it was at times difficult to be certain what President Kennedy would finally do. As one who knew him well says: "He reacted to everyone in a different way; one can only judge him by the decisions he reached in the end." Those who worked for him differ sharply on whether he would have followed more or less the same policy that President Johnson pursued in Vietnam. Even before he became President, Kennedy made some speeches stressing the importance of Southeast Asia. It would not have been easy for him to buck the prevailing mood in Congress: the accusation against the Democrats that they had "lost China" was still echoing. After the Bay of Pigs, too, he wanted to prove that he was not afraid to resist Communist pressures. He had an opportunity, when General Taylor and Walt Rostow presented their report, either to opt out or to make an all-out commitment; but he did neither, accepting half their prescription. They had qualms about the lack of leadership in Diem's government, but felt this could be made up by injecting American advisers into the operation. The Pentagon at that point was not keen on sending troops to Vietnam, and the President made a conscious decision against doing so.

One reason why I think he would not have followed, as stubbornly and steadfastly, the same course as Mr.

Johnson is that he was a more temperate, more prag-
matic man, neither as dogged and unyielding as Johnson nor as prestige-conscious. He would also have been
more impatient with the political instability of the
Saigon regime; he might well have decided that since
the American objective was to help the South Vietnamese to help themselves, and since they were incapable
of doing so, he might justifiably disengage from the war.
It was never clearly stated that the U.S. would pull out
if it became evident that the political structure was so
weak that nothing more could be done to bolster it, but
it was implicit in the terms of his commitment. Secretary of State Dean Rusk, however, held the stricter view
that the SEATO Treaty obliged the U.S. to defend
South Vietnam.

Equally, one could argue that Kennedy's advisers
would have led him in the same direction they led Johnson. But there was good reason to think that Kennedy
would have replaced Rusk as Secretary of State, and
Walt Rostow would not have been at the President's
elbow. He was shunted by Kennedy to the Planning
Staff of the State Department in late 1961 ("Walt has
ten ideas every day," said Kennedy, "nine of which
would lead to disaster but one of which is worth having,
and this makes it important to have a filter between the
President and Rostow"). Rostow, as he often said, based
his view on the contention that "the North Vietnamese
have violated their solemn obligation to withdraw from

South Vietnam and from Laos given in 1954 and 1963, and for that they must be punished."

McGeorge Bundy, Kennedy's adviser on Security Affairs, remained convinced for some time that it would be possible to force Hanoi to the conference table, but during his time with Johnson I often had the feeling that he stuck to this policy both because he believed in it and out of the sense of honor, loyalty, and steadfastness learned in his Groton schooldays. He still continues, with the reticence acquired from his old mentor Henry Stimson (Franklin Roosevelt's Secretary of War), to avoid criticizing Johnson.

Kennedy's Secretary of Defense, Robert McNamara, also held the view for a long time that an attempt had to be made to win the war. He was convinced that there was a way of doing it. He always assumed that the military did not know much about planning and budgeting or about programming and cost-effectiveness, but he was surprised when they did not seem to know how to fight this war. He did not try to press his own ideas on military strategy; he once told me that he left this to the military because it was a field in which he did not feel sufficiently competent.

But to be fair one must also take into consideration that one of Kennedy's most far-reaching decisions was to abandon the Eisenhower theory of massive retaliation and replace it with the "flexible response." The idea was that in the nuclear age, when the balance of terror made wars between super-powers unlikely, the U.S., to contain Communist aggression, had to equip itself with the tools to fight limited wars. In a sweeping intellectual reorientation, McNamara began training and equipping American and Vietnamese Special Forces. The Americans were to fight local insurgencies anywhere in the world, and Vietnam became their first test. The Kennedy team hoped to prove the validity of their ideas; it was another factor that made it so difficult for them to admit that their limited-war calculations had been misconceived, at least in the political and military swamps of Vietnam.

Kennedy assumed that the war was going well in 1961 and 1962, but at the end of 1962, in a conversation with Roswell Gilpatrick, he talked in a restless and impatient way about how the U.S. had been sucked into Vietnam little by little. By the autumn of 1963 he seemed sick of it, and frequently asked how to be rid of the commitment. He began talking about the need to reduce the size of American forces in Europe and extricate the U.S. from Southeast Asia. Just before his death he gave Mike Forrestal, in private conversation, odds of a hundred-to-one that the U.S. could not win. But he also knew that he could not get out of Vietnam before the elections in November, 1964, without inviting his own political eclipse. In a way, the Green Beret that lies on his grave in Arlington Cemetery is the symbol not only of individual heroism but also of a major miscalculation in war and politics.

II

Johnson:

The Snares of Continuity

Early in 1964 a complete reassessment of America's commitment in Vietnam would have been possible. Instead, the war that summer moved into a new phase and the commitment deepened. Understandably, President Johnson's opening policy theme was "Let us continue"; and just as he inherited the Kennedy policies, so also the presidential elections still loomed ahead. Both considerations made it politically impossible for any change of course in Vietnam.

There, eighteen months of political chaos began on January 30, 1964, with yet another coup in Saigon. Major General Nguyen Khanh, who later became outspokenly anti-American, ousted Major General Duong Van Minh. For this chaotic situation Johnson blamed the fall of Diem (whom he once called "an Asian Churchill") and those who had brought it about.

Robert McNamara, the Secretary of Defense, in a speech before the House Armed Services Committee on January 27, declared that the situation was "grave," but that "the survival of an independent government in

South Vietnam is so important to the security of Southeast Asia and to the free world that I can conceive of no alternative other than to take the necessary measures within our capability to prevent a Communist victory."

Then, in May, Dean Rusk, the Secretary of State, who found President Johnson more congenial to deal with than Kennedy, warned that "if Communists persist in their course of aggression" the war might have to be expanded. Senator William Fulbright, Chairman of the Senate Foreign Relations Committee, still agreed in those days with Mr. Rusk that "the U.S. bargaining position was weak and that until the equation of advantage between the two sides had been substantially altered in our favor there could be little prospect of a negotiated settlement." The President for his part gave general instructions to keep the war in a low key and avoid controversial initiatives that could upset the election campaign.

But there is a limit to the extent to which even an American President can control events. The theme song of Mr. Johnson's election speeches was his aim for a peaceful solution in Vietnam, and the contrast he created to his Republican opponent Senator Barry Goldwater's bellicose speeches gave him a growing political advantage. The North Vietnamese, however, almost succeeded in upsetting the Johnson campaign strategy when on August 2, 1964, their gunboats attacked the U.S. destroyer *Maddox*. It was only an incident, but it gave impetus to the advocates of the need to bomb the "sanctuary" of North Vietnam. When five months later their views prevailed, it was also shown that the U.S. was wrong to fear Chinese or Russian retaliation: the U.S. could "get away with it."

First news of the Tonkin incident reached Washington early on Sunday morning. Those who were awakened by the duty officer at the State Department could not get through to Dean Rusk on the telephone. His air conditioner was apparently noisier than the bell of his telephone in the room next to his bedroom (he insisted on keeping it there so as to make it necessary for him to get up and walk to the phone, thus ensuring that by the time he lifted the receiver he would be fully awake). By 6 A.M., however, General Earle Wheeler, Chairman of the Joint Chiefs of Staff, Cyrus Vance, Deputy Secretary of Defense, and Tom Hughes, Assistant Secretary for Intelligence and Research, were at Rusk's house to brief him on the attack. Then they went on to tell the President.

Johnson did not seem perturbed. He was much more concerned with a postal bill, and for a long hour he treated his early-morning guests to a recital of the intricacies of getting that bill through Congress. He finished without further mention of the *Maddox* and the Tonkin incident. But two days later, when the North Vietnamese gunboats struck again, the President did not want to show weakness before repeated provocation, either to Hanoi or to the American electorate in the last weeks of the election campaign. He ordered instant retaliation against the boat pens in North Vietnam. He was determined to teach Ho Chi Minh a lesson.

The following day he sent his Southeast Asia resolution to Congress, seeking special powers "to take all necessary measures to repel any armed attack against the forces of the U.S. and to prevent further aggression." It was adopted within two days, but in the years that followed, it alienated many in Congress, who came to feel that the President's powers were far too broad. And in fact the second attack was not in itself very important: in the view of some high Pentagon officials, "We overreacted."

The second attack had a much greater impact on American public opinion than the first, and Johnson's reaction reflected his concern about the effect it would have on the election campaign: he felt he had to make a show of strength. His speeches assumed a sharper, more militant tone, although they were still balanced by his assurances that he did not want a policy of "constant conflict, rising hostility, and deepening tension." He did not want to spoil his winning peace issue against Senator Goldwater, who let himself be pictured as an irrational warmonger.

But in South Vietnam, according to an intelligence field report, the first bombing of North Vietnamese installations registered only equivocal support. None of the twenty-five South Vietnamese, for instance, who were overheard in conversation amongst themselves by an American intelligence agent, indicated any particular disapproval of the North Vietnamese attacks on American ships. And almost all those who disapproved of American bombing did so because Americans were now unilaterally killing Vietnamese, while in the past they had merely helped Vietnamese kill Vietnamese. Small as this sample of opinion was, the report nevertheless explains much about the psyche of the Vietnamese and their attitude toward the war and Americans.

Three and a half years later, the Tonkin incident became the subject of a Senate investigation. And in early 1968, suspicions of experts were aroused when, on the anniversary of the attack, the North Vietnamese decorated their sailors for the *first* incident, but the citation did not mention the second.

President Johnson won the election in November, 1964, with an overwhelming mandate. He was at the peak of his strength. At that moment he could have carried through almost any decision. But his top advisers presented an almost solid front in favor of the prosecution of the war and against "scuttling with honor." The only opposition came from Vice-President Hubert Humphrey, George Ball, Under Secretary of State, and some people at sub-Cabinet level. They argued that for ten years Vietnam had tested American patience, and that this was now an opportune moment to disengage. What they should have pressed for then was a major diplomatic offensive for negotiations.

General de Gaulle, in those days in particular, was a

thorn in the side of the U.S. He thoroughly opposed the war and said so. The U.S. hoped to restrain his opposition by being polite to him, and so George Ball went to Paris. In the fifties, Ball had represented the French Government as a lawyer, and in that role had lived through the French agony in Indochina. Now he presented the official view to the General: the American alternatives were to build a strong government in Saigon to which people would rally, or to exert enough military pressure on the North to discourage the promotion of insurrection in the South.

De Gaulle disagreed. He favored a large conference of all the interested countries within the area, the aim of which would be the neutralization of Southeast Asia. He believed that once such a conference got under way, Ho Chi Minh would put a halt to the war and gradually the problem of Vietnam could be submerged within the problems of the entire area. Such a conference, he thought, might last a year or two. He did not regard China as an expansionist power, and he was also convinced that Ho Chi Minh and the North Vietnamese Government had inherited the ancient Indochinese determination to resist Chinese domination. What worried him was that the U.S., with its involvement in the war, was risking Chinese intervention.

France, de Gaulle said, had found Vietnam a "rotten country"; the U.S. would, too, and would therefore find it impossible to win the war. He agreed that the U.S. had more power to bring to bear than France, but he insisted that the power to destroy the entire country would still not enable the United States to win. All the U.S. could achieve would be to maintain a massive presence.

Ball, a man with personal style, strong convictions, and the gift of advocacy, had been for some time the most articulate opponent of the war within the Administration. On October 5, 1964, he sent a long memorandum to Dean Rusk, McGeorge Bundy, the President's adviser on National Security Affairs, and Robert McNamara, in which he argued that the Saigon Government could neither provide a solid center for the broad support of the Vietnamese people nor conduct military operations to clean up the insurgency. Instead he recommended a course of action that would permit a political settlement without direct U.S. military involvement, under conditions that would be designed to check or delay the extension of Communist power into South Vietnam by giving maximum protection to Thailand, Malaysia, and Southeast Asia, and thus minimize the damage to U.S. prestige.

To those (such as Dean Rusk) who often mentioned the experiences of Munich and Korea as a warning and fitting analogy for intercession in Vietnam, he retorted that in Korea the U.S. was under a clear United Nations mandate, with the support of 54,000 soldiers from other countries; the Syngman Rhee Government was stable— two years after their new-found independence Koreans were still enthusiastic about it; and the Korean War had begun with an overt massive land invasion from the North, whereas in Vietnam the Vietcong insurgency had indigenous support.

But Ball's memo had little impact. He gradually became known as "the devil's advocate." He was listened to, he helped make people think again, and occasionally he worried the President; in the Johnson Administration he was tolerated as society often tolerates eccentrics. Ball's principal ally was Llewellyn Thompson, both in Washington and as U.S. Ambassador in Moscow. They believed strongly that the key to the international power struggle lay in Europe; both the President and Dean Rusk thought it had shifted to Asia.

Rusk's whole outlook was fashioned when he was a staff planner in the Asian theater during the Second World War. He did not get on well with his British colleagues there, and it left a legacy. As a former Rhodes scholar he retained a warm feeling for Oxford, though, and when he could, he attended the annual Oxford-Cambridge boat-race dinner in Washington. When occasionally he delivered the speech of the evening, he would display the quiet wit that enabled him still to blend easily with that very special collegiate audience.

He went through the trials of the Korean War as an Assistant Secretary in the State Department, and later he took a strongly emotional view that Vietnam, like Korea, was a test of all U.S. world commitments. The military at the Pentagon regarded him as more of an ally than McNamara and his civilian whiz kids. Sometimes his detractors said that he had turned the State Department into an adjunct of the Joint Chiefs of Staff.

Rusk's impassive facial expression and his almost infinite patience concealed both passion and strong, unbending convictions. He deeply resented Britain's failure to join the U.S. in the fight in Vietnam, and time and again in private he taunted me with remarks like "Why don't you write an article about your government's failure to live up to its SEATO Treaty commitment?" But as George Ball once pointed out to the President (in a memorandum on February 12, 1966), the SEATO Treaty, when read together with its protocol, does not commit the U.S. to the South Vietnamese people or government. "Our only treaty commitment in that area is to the SEATO partners, and they have without exception viewed the situation in Vietnam as not calling the Treaty into play. To be sure, we did make a promise to the South Vietnamese people. But that promise was conditional on their own performance and they have not performed." This was Ball's interpretation, and he used to be a high-priced lawyer. Others besides Dean Rusk (such as William Bundy) disagreed with this interpretation.

Mr. Rusk also used to say that the French in 1954 had sold out, that they lost the war not in Vietnam but in Paris, and he always insisted that he would not have it said that the war was lost in Washington.

Despite their differences, he and George Ball were on good terms. Toward the end of the day they would exchange ideas and "chew the fat" over a glass of whiskey in Rusk's office. Rusk was an extraordinarily tolerant man, except on Vietnam. This was his field of honor, and on it he staked all he had. It was his passion to the extent of being an affliction. It was to him the supreme test of the American will.

After the election President Johnson never seriously considered using his new, big mandate to disengage from Vietnam; on the contrary, he got inflated ideas of what he could accomplish. He was misled into feeling that Congress and the country were behind him. Bill Moyers, his onetime Press Secretary, was convinced that the President in his own mind was committed to winning. And certainly public and congressional opinion, too, were then still backing the war.

The discrepancy between Johnson's real feelings and those he had expressed during the election campaign must have led Hanoi into misjudging his inclinations and intentions. This may have been the largest and most misleading credibility gap. From then on, his words probably carried little conviction with Ho Chi Minh. If Hanoi expected some sort of peace talks with the newly elected President, it was badly mistaken.

In South Vietnam the political and military situation was deteriorating as more assistance flowed in from the North, and in almost the same ratio President Johnson's will to resist was being stiffened. In Washington, talk behind the scenes about bombing the "sanctuary" gained momentum.

Already, at the Honolulu meeting in 1964, some of the younger planners had suggested pinpointed retaliatory bombing of the North for everything the Vietcong committed in the South. The Saigon military command and the Pacific Command CINCPAC opposed this idea; they wanted heavy bombardment. They argued that unless the bombing was done soon and fast, the enemy would have time to improve his antiaircraft defenses. Johnson later said that "North Vietnam ought to be touched up a bit," and it may be that by then he was already thinking of changing the nature of the war and the American commitment.

The Joint Chiefs of Staff proposed that bombing be started by hitting the airfields around Hanoi. Both McNamara and General Taylor objected, partly for moral reasons and partly because they wanted to test their theory of "flexible response," which involved not a heavy bombardment but a series of attacks north of the Demilitarized Zone. Their theory was that if you twist someone's arm he can "cry uncle," but if you go for his neck from the beginning he doesn't get the chance. The moral restraints that they also felt underline how different the conflict in Vietnam is from the Second World War, in which almost anything in the way of bombing was permissible. Limited wars have their great frustrations for the military.

41

There was also the risk that complete devastation of North Vietnam might bring China into the war, just as had happened in Korea (a few of the military itched for an opportunity to "hit" China, but this was never seriously considered). The Air Force view was that it was operating under heavy handicaps, so it was not surprising that it pressed for being allowed to hit the jugular —even though this did not exist in Vietnam because of the few industrial targets.

In September, the Joint War Games Agency of the Joint Chiefs of Staff, after one of their frolics, proved that even when everything on the then-proposed list of air-strike targets had been ticked off, Hanoi would still be capable of increasing its shipment of supplies to the South. Some in the Administration challenged the premise that it would be easier to negotiate with North Vietnam after an air offensive: they thought it was based on a wrong assessment of the worldwide political impact of bombing, and the effect this would have on America's bargaining power. Others, including George Ball, warned that escalation by air power would induce the North Vietnamese to send in more ground forces, of which they had plenty, and to increase terror and sabotage in the South. But all the warnings were ignored.

The great policy review in late 1964, according to William Bundy, Assistant Secretary of State, showed that it was impractical to continue the current policy. There were only two courses open to the U.S.—move toward withdrawal, or do a lot more, both for military advantage and to prevent a collapse of South Vietnamese morale and will to continue. Neither choice was very appealing. Those who favored withdrawal no doubt argued that the U.S. commitment had lapsed since the South Vietnamese were unable to help themselves, in spite of all the American help provided thus far. The most fallacious theory (as it became clear later on), so convincingly presented at that time to President Johnson, was the idea that the application of graduated force would make the North Vietnamese "hurt" so much that they would abandon the South.

Withdrawal itself offered an option: either to "beat it" unilaterally, or to seek some sort of face-saving device through talks.

A private attempt by U.N. Secretary-General U Thant to initiate negotiations did not appeal to Mr. Johnson. U Thant had been critical of the U.S. and charitable about what the North Vietnamese were doing, and he was therefore not considered a desirable interlocutor. When he sent a message that Ho Chi Minh would be willing to meet the Americans quietly in Rangoon, it was assumed in Washington that he had indicated to Hanoi that the Americans were ready to surrender. His proposal was not only vague, but also came at a time when Washington was all too conscious of the impending collapse of the South Vietnamese. In addition, it was never seriously pressed (according to one of his aides) by Mr. Adlai Stevenson, the American Ambassador to the United Nations, through whom U

Thant communicated with Washington. Scarcely any record of these exchanges exists; it seems that Mr. Stevenson discussed the suggestion with Mr. Rusk by telephone, rather than in diplomatic dispatches, and Rusk behaved as if it had never been mentioned.

When I met Mr. Stevenson in New York in February, 1965, he was upset about the course of the war and unhappy about how little influence he had on decisions. What troubled him most was how badly the Johnson Administration had handled its public relations. He showed me a memo to the President proposing more publicity for the various offers of negotiations and peace feelers that the U.S. had made, so as to emphasize their failure through the uncompromising attitude of Hanoi. He told the President that he should do more to "put the monkey" on the enemy's back.

Stevenson also mentioned the U Thant initiative. He told me he had transmitted it to Washington, and complained that there had been no reply until it was too late. U Thant had repeated the offer in December, and Stevenson had had to tell him on February 5 that Washington had rejected the idea.

U Thant's view, conveyed to me later, was that Stevenson had probably assumed in the first place that nothing could be done until after the November elections. But more probably it was simply felt that the offer had come from the wrong quarter at the wrong time. The Saigon Government was then in such political and military disarray that the majority in Washington

44

believed that if the U.S. had sat down with Hanoi at the negotiating table, it would soon have had no government in Saigon to negotiate for.

In any event, the whole affair was finally discounted when a high Soviet source indicated to Dean Rusk that it was based on a remark by the Russian delegate to the United Nations, which U Thant had misunderstood.

There was another reason for American wariness over talks. A high-ranking U.S. official recently put it to me this way: "The trouble was that hints from Hanoi came through self-appointed 'missionaries'—people we did not consider reliable, such as American pacifists, South Asian politicians, Mexican Nobel-prize aspirants, Italian socialists, French Foreign Office officials. I exclude U Thant from this group. They never sent a guy around to tell us that they wanted to negotiate. They never took the initiative."

The North Vietnamese failure to take this initiative annoyed, mystified, and exasperated American officials. Considering the weakness in Saigon, an overt offer could easily have brought down any South Vietnamese government. But Asian Communists have their own ways, their own pride, their own prejudices and suspicions. They probably did not trust American assurances that the U.S. meant to withdraw its troops from Vietnam. Above all they must have assumed, if the American assessment of the situation in the South was correct, that the plum would fall into their lap one day soon, that all they had to do was wait. Up to a point, they assessed the American attitude correctly. The U.S. did not want to enter talks with a weak hand; and it was equally confident that time was on its side. For both, the line was "Let's wait a little longer and we'll be in a better position to negotiate." Somehow the position was never quite good enough.

To those Americans who wanted to get out of Vietnam, unilateral action was preferable to face-saving talks. But withdrawal was something that President Johnson himself was unwilling to contemplate. He once said to me, "I'm not going to be the first American President to lose a war." Simply to carry on as things stood was bound to lead to defeat; the U.S. had to make some sort of escalatory move. A new element had to be introduced, and that element was bombing. When, on February 7, 1965, three attacks occurred against U.S. and South Vietnamese installations (the most important being Pleiku), they easily triggered the decision. American bombers hit back at the North the same day.

III

Fallacies of Escalation

The bombing opened an entirely new chapter in the war. The instant retaliation to the Pleiku attacks was recommended by McGeorge Bundy and John McNaughton, then Assistant Secretary for International Security Affairs at the Pentagon, for three reasons: first, to bolster the Saigon Government's low morale; second, to avenge the outrages against American soldiers; and third, to impress the South Vietnamese people with the seriousness of American intentions in the hope that this would make them choose the American side. The code name for the offensive—which by March it had become—was "Rolling Thunder": nobody suspected how apt it would prove to be. Everybody underestimated the rolling momentum of escalation; it was assumed that the President could put an end to the bombing anytime he wanted to. Neither public opinion nor the military was going to give him that free a hand.

Few could see the dynamism inherent in escalation. It becomes a state of mind. Some of the most rational men in the Administration were misled by the thought, "Just a little more and we will turn the corner." It was one of the great fallacies of the war, but it took a long time, as we shall see, for that fact to be grasped. Just as in the other fallacy—that bombing would hurt the North so much that it would abandon the South—no consideration was given (though it was pointed out by Ball) to the way in which bombing would impel the United States to increase its ground forces. Escalation cost a great deal not only in manpower and money, but also in terms of social cohesion within the United States.

In May, 1965, two marine battalions were sent to Vietnam, the first U.S. *combat* units to be deployed there. By June the U.S. military authorities disclosed that their personnel had passed the 50,000 mark. By June 16 the total was raised to 70,000.

In Europe there was suddenly fear of a wider war, and in Washington a decision had to be taken whether or not to continue punishment from the skies. President Johnson told one of his principal ambassadors: "I must show the Vietnamese and Chinese that they cannot play games with the U.S., that we are not a paper tiger. I will retaliate and carry out deterrent action, but I won't do the wild stuff some of my military are advocating. They tell me I can destroy everything the Russians and the Chinese can bring into play. And I won't send ground troops." The ambassador's comment later was, "He's a tornado translated into words."

Washington in the spring of 1965 steeled itself for a further intensification of the war. What made it all a little eerie for the people there was the feeling that they were moving about blindfolded, for the President imposed almost unparalleled secrecy. For a man who liked to be presented with as many options as possible, his were now more and more limited. He was caught in the updraft of escalation.

Something close to a consensus now existed among his key advisers that there was little left to do but step up the war—the alternative being ignominious withdrawal, with all its dire consequences for the American power position in the Pacific. The decision to bomb the North on a regular basis, however, was not acted on until it had become clear, in March, that British efforts to reconvene the Geneva Conference of 1954 had been turned down by the Soviet Union.

The decision to bomb the North without waiting for specific provocation brought great satisfaction to Walt Rostow, who was still in the State Department. He had always favored a policy of intimidation, and the decision finally supported the view he had held from the beginning. The belief that there was a dignified "soft" option for fighting the war was to him a delusion; he regarded it as impossible to win a guerrilla war as long as the enemy enjoyed the advantage of an open frontier between North and South. He had always felt that a penalty had to be imposed for aggression, and the sooner the better. Others, especially among the military, agreed with him that had the U.S. begun with the determination that it was now beginning to display, the war would already have been over, and to America's advantage.

In late 1964 the U.S. Intelligence Community—the combined arms of U.S. intelligence—had unanimously agreed that in the event of an American attack above the Nineteenth Parallel, Chinese aircraft "would probably" operate from Chinese bases to assist North Vietnam. But by February, 1965, this estimate had been scaled down to "might occur": the State Department's China experts and George Ball consistently overrated the risk of Chinese intervention.

Unhappily, the first bombardment of North Vietnam coincided with the visit of Mr. Kosygin to Hanoi. This was not an error of judgment, as was widely suspected at the time, but happened because everybody was frantic that retaliation for Pleiku not be postponed for fear of its becoming indefinitely delayed or losing its symbolic significance.

George Ball, who at the time was acting Secretary of State, supported the decision to bomb, though he had grave misgivings about it. Both he and Vice-President Humphrey opposed the timing: they thought it highly provocative to begin bombing while Kosygin was in Hanoi. But Ball gave his support because he was afraid of losing all credibility; he felt that as the "devil's advocate" he was still playing a useful role, but one that depended on his staying in his job and retaining the President's trust in him and his loyalty. Some thought he was trying to have it both ways. Humphrey, for opposing the bombing altogether, was "punished" by exclusion from the decision-making processes of the war (though not from the unimportant deliberations in the National Security Council) for almost a whole year.

Walt Rostow shrugged off the importance of Kosygin's visit and the damage involved in the bombing's coinciding with it. He said that Kosygin had not gone to Hanoi to persuade the North Vietnamese to make peace, but to be "in on the kill" because the situation looked so favorable from Hanoi's point of view. Kosygin's trip did, however, result in a decision to give more defense assistance to Hanoi. U.S. intelligence estimates then made it an even chance that this would include ground-to-air missiles with Russian crews.

To most of the President's advisers, the problem facing the U.S. was how to prevent defeat and bring the enemy to accept negotiations on reasonable terms. George Ball and Ambassador Llewellyn Thompson gave Mr. Johnson this analysis of the situation as they saw it: Hanoi would never abandon the aggressive course it had pursued at great cost for ten years, and give up all the progress made in the communization of South Vietnam. For North Vietnam to call off the insurgency in the South, close the border, and withdraw the elements it had infiltrated into South Vietnam would be to accept unconditional surrender. Furthermore, China would be extremely reluctant to permit Hanoi to submit to such a surrender, because it would mean the collapse of the basic Chinese ideological position, which was in conflict with the Russians'. The Chinese would then be under great pressure to engage the U.S. both on the ground and in the air; the risk of their intervention would be great, and its cost tremendous.

Both men pointed out that they had supported the air strikes so far, and would also support a program of gradually increasing military pressure, because they believed that only in that way could the U.S. achieve a bargaining position that would then lead to some acceptable international arrangement that avoided humiliating defeat. They did not believe, however, that the U.S. could realistically hope for international arrangements that would effectively stop the insurrection in South Vietnam and deliver the entire country south of the Seventeenth Parallel to the government in Saigon.

The most the U.S. could realistically hope for from any international arrangement, they thought, would be measures to stop infiltration so that it might, over a period, reduce its commitments. Hopefully, they said, the military actions preceding such an arrangement would have created sufficient sense of unity in Saigon to make it possible for the government there (with diminishing U.S. help) to clean up an insurgency that would be made manageable by the closing of the border.

Robert McNamara and McGeorge Bundy took a different view. They believed that the U.S. must continue to increase military pressure to the point where Hanoi was prepared to agree not only to stop infiltration, but also effectively to call off the insurgency and withdraw those elements infiltrated in the past. To achieve this objective they would accept the risk of substantial escalation.

To balance this new upward trend, the President was persuaded to make his so-called Baltimore speech on April 7, 1965, in which he offered Hanoi "unconditional discussions" to prove that the U.S. was not bent on military victory. According to Walter Lippmann, the noted columnist, who was then still on good terms with the President, the draft Mr. Johnson showed him before delivery did not contain this offer, and it may be that it was added after Mr. Lippmann complained that the President was swinging the stick but offering no carrot, no indication for the basis of a peaceful settlement. The speech contained an offer to build a power dam on the Mekong River, yet also some of the toughest justification for America's part in the war: "Over this war—and all Asia—is another reality: the deepening shadow of Communist China. . . . The contest in Vietnam is part of a wider pattern of aggressive purposes. We are there because we have a promise to keep. . . ." There was no response from Hanoi, except a snarl.

On April 21, George Ball sent the President an unusually impassioned and prophetic memorandum. It began with a warning that an appeal for a negotiated peace, by seventeen nonaligned nations on April 1, represented a feeler that should not be ignored. What moved him to write was the specter of large-scale escalation "that would multiply the dangers and American responsibilities, transform the character of the war, increase American casualties, and induce Hanoi to step up the rate of infiltration."

By then the U.S. had mounted 2,800 bombing sorties, increasing in intensity from 122 per week in early February to 664 per week in mid-April. Some thirty-two targets in North Vietnam had been damaged or destroyed, and yet there was no evidence to show that infiltration had even been slowed down.

"We cannot continue to bomb the North and use napalm against South Vietnamese villages without progressive erosion of our world position," Ball wrote. "Until now the American people have gone along out of their great confidence in you and because U.S. casualties have been less than a weekend's traffic accidents. But even doubling of the casualties would begin to make a difference."

Ball then argued in favor of using the declaration of the seventeen nonaligned nations to open negotiations, since the President had already offered "unconditional discussions"; at the same time the U.S. would make clear that the basis for an ultimate settlement must be "an independent and neutral South Vietnam, securely guaranteed and able to shape its own relationship to all others, free from outside interference, tied to no alliances, a military base for no other country."

Hanoi's position was based on a four-point proposal

which, Ball argued, was like the American position in that it also demanded total capitulation by the other side. In analyzing Hanoi's four points, he suggested that the U.S. could agree to recognize the "basic initial rights of the Vietnamese people—peace, sovereignty, unity, territorial integrity; agree to return to peaceful reunification of Vietnam; agree that internal affairs of South Vietnam must be settled by the South Vietnamese themselves." He accepted that there were aspects of the plan to which the U.S. could not agree, but concluded: "We will ultimately have to settle for an arrangement under which the National Liberation Front would be given the opportunity, along with other political parties, to campaign freely but without the use of terror or intimidation for political support among the South Vietnamese people."

But Ball's views (close to the American position as presented at the Paris peace talks in 1969) were running ahead of events. In 1965, the belief that any Saigon government would collapse and thus almost automatically open the way for a Communist takeover ruled out Ball's plan; no one considered it seriously.

On May 6, the first two reinforced marine battalions were sent to Vietnam to be put ashore for "limited duty." They were only a foot in the door, but they were the first organized American combat units to be sent into the fighting; their duty was defined by Dean Rusk as providing "local, close-in security." In early June it became known that 50,000 troops were available for combat duty. The Administration began to prepare the public for a larger American role in the war, and larger casualties. By then it had become clear that South Vietnam was near military collapse; an entire South Vietnamese battalion, for example, had simply defected. Late in June began the most far-reaching review of the war.

On July 10, President Johnson again avowed his determination: "We committed our power and our honor and that has been reaffirmed by three Presidents." However great an exaggeration that was, it heralded the escalation to come. It is clear that Mr. Johnson was in no doubt about the need to escalate the war—what remained to be decided was how much. Joseph Califano, who later became the President's Chief Administrative Assistant but at that time was working for Secretary McNamara, coordinated some eleven different options for escalation. McNamara flew out to Saigon for six days, and on his return on July 20 declared: "In many respects there has been a deterioration in the Vietnam War." He recommended to the President an increase from 50,000 to 150,000 men, and preparations to go up to 200,000. His memorandum acknowledged that they might be faced with the same demand yet again the following year, but unless they acted now, he said, South Vietnam would fall.

It was a choice between two evils. It meant in effect that the U.S. would have to assume virtually full responsibility for the war. The plan that was drawn up included call-up of the reserves and requests to Congress for such large new funds and such broad powers that the plan amounted more or less to a declaration of war. This last the President had always skirted, because it would have meant a basic departure from the American goal of helping protect South Vietnam from Communist aggression, and instead implied the total destruction of North Vietnam.

For about a week the President fretted over this plan. He concluded that if he went that far it could very well wreck his Great Society program. He therefore asked McNamara for a revised plan that would cost less and make call-up of the reserves unnecessary. On July 26, the new plan became policy by unanimous recommendation. It provided for an increase to 150,000 men and, if necessary, more.

While Johnson fretted, he had before him another memorandum from the "devil's advocate," written on June 18, in which Ball said:

> Ralph Waldo Emerson once wrote: "Things are in the saddle, and ride mankind."
>
> In monsoon period I recommend that we decide now to authorize an increase of American forces in Vietnam to an aggregate level of 100,000, but no more additional forces to deal with Vietcong offensive during rainy season.
>
> Instruct Secretary of State and Defense:
> 1) that you are not committing U.S. forces on open-ended basis to an all-out land war in South Vietnam;

2) that instead you are making a controlled commitment for a trial period of three months;

3) that on that trial period basis we will appraise the costs and possibilities of waging a successful land war.

It means *new* war, U.S. against Vietcong. Perhaps the large-scale introduction of American forces with their concentrated firepower will force Hanoi and the Vietcong to the decision we are seeking. On the other hand, we may *not* be able to fight the war successfully enough even with 500,000 Americans in South Vietnam to achieve this purpose.

A review of the French experience more than a decade ago may be helpful. The French fought a war in Vietnam and were finally defeated—after seven years of bloody struggle and when they still had 250,000 combat-hardened veterans in the field supported by an army of 205,000 South Vietnamese. To be sure, the French were fighting a colonial war while we are fighting to stop aggression. But when we have put enough Americans on the ground in South Vietnam to give the appearance of a white man's war, the distinctions as to our ultimate purpose will have less and less practical effect. Nor is our position in Vietnam without its historical ambiguities. From 1948–54 we identified ourselves with the French by providing almost *four billion of U.S. aid to help* the French in Indochina wage war against the Viet Minh. Today no one can say for certain how many Vietnamese are for us or against us.

Ever since 1961 we have met successive disappointments. We have tended to underestimate the strength and staying power of the enemy. We have tended to overestimate the effectiveness of our sophisticated weapons under jungle conditions. We have been unable to bring about the creation of a stable political base in Saigon. The French had much the same experience. But we have things running for us that the French did not have.

In terms of escalation, July, 1965, was the most crucial period of the war. Nobody quite knows what went on in the President's mind as he communed with himself for almost a week about this fateful decision. He had to weigh all the political consequences of going ahead and not going ahead. Defeat was unthinkable; victory now loomed larger as the goal. When Johnson finally decided in favor of escalation, he had no doubt that he had made the right decision.

Yet for the first time in its history the U.S. was fighting a war to negotiate a political settlement. This is a highly sophisticated course for the greatest power to take, and not an easy one for an impatient, power-conscious President. This is why he later seemed to waver between seeking "the coonskin cap" and wanting to get negotiations started. One of his oldest friends remarked to me at the time: "Johnson is a consensus man when he can see two objectives between which to seek a compromise. He becomes a power man when he can't see both. Then he sets out to impose his will. The danger then is that if he gets a bloody nose he will get even more stubborn and hit back even harder."

The American effort gained enormous momentum. At least one of the principal architects of this escalation now believes that it was a mistake, that a holding operation might have been enough gradually to bring the foe to the conference table. The majority of those responsible for the decision, and certainly President Johnson, still believe that they had no alternative. But once the U.S. assumed full control of the war, the policymakers began to realize that there existed a vital kinetic relationship between the war and the internal political situation in Vietnam. Nobody thought at this stage that this would also apply to the United States, both to its internal political situation and in terms of serious inflationary pressures.

Shortly before the end of the Johnson Administration, I suggested to Dean Rusk that one of his influential colleagues (not Mr. Ball) now believed that they might have pulled back if someone had said, as President Kennedy did during the Cuban missile crisis: "It isn't the first step that concerns me, but both sides escalating to the fourth and fifth step . . . we are embarking on a very hazardous course." Mr. Rusk is celebrated for his bland replies, and has some reputation as a phrasemaker ("They were facing each other eyeball to eyeball"; or, about running for political office, "You have to expose yourself from gizzard to guts"). On this occasion he looked at me for long seconds, and then said decisively, "Horseshit."

But it was not simply that nobody tried to see where escalation would lead. The Intelligence Community provided a plethora of estimates. Yet most of the time there was a difference between the general estimates of the Central Intelligence Agency and the Military Intelligence. Military estimates were usually much more optimistic than the CIA's, and as optimism proved increasingly misleading, so the Administration (including the Secretary of Defense) tended to rely more on CIA reporting. Its most valuable contribution to the war was its accurate assessment (in contrast to Air Force claims) of the real effects of the bombing in the North—the CIA virtually discounted the effect of the bombing of Haiphong on the flow of materiel into the South.

The CIA also made a contribution to the training of the "counterrevolutionary" forces which helped to protect villages and the pacification efforts. But its information on impending political coups in Saigon, and its predictions of enemy intentions, were unreliable. One of the worst blunders of the Intelligence Community was its failure to predict the Tet offensive in 1968.

Several key members of the Johnson Administration complain in retrospect that intelligence about the nature of the enemy was highly inadequate, and that there were few predictions that the North Vietnamese would have the stamina they proved to have. Those responsible deny this, claiming that they gave ample warning. Another complaint is about a great lack of information concerning the National Liberation Front and the Vietcong. Many South Vietnamese families had relatives in the NLF, yet there was a dearth, if not an absence, of real intelligence channels to them. An organization as mobile and dedicated as the NLF, and without a fixed center, is always difficult to infiltrate.

Nobody really knew where it would all lead, how far escalation itself would have to go. Nobody had much confidence in the leadership of General Ky, now President of South Vietnam. There was only one certainty —that Mr. Johnson was a man unlikely to allow himself to be humiliated.

In the hope that the new commitment would, however, help to intimidate Hanoi and make it readier to negotiate, a secret channel of communications was opened through what is called a trusted official emissary. But by the end of October it had become obvious that the kind of offers made by the State Department held no temptations for Hanoi, that it still insisted, unacceptably, on recognition of the NLF as "the sole representative of the people of South Vietnam." The Russians claimed that they did not know what Hanoi's views were. And American troops in South Vietnam climbed to 150,000.

Several key figures in the Administration, however, were not satisfied with the October feeler and began to press the President for an experimental pause in the bombing. The idea developed late in November in anticipation of the Christmas truce. Its advocates were McNamara; McGeorge Bundy; his brother Bill, the Assistant Secretary for Far Eastern Affairs; Bill Moyers; Joseph Califano, who had now become the President's

Chief Administrative Assistant; and Cyrus Vance, Deputy Secretary of Defense. With the idea came, on November 27, a march of from 15,000 to 35,000 people on the White House in protest against the war.

Dean Rusk exerted himself neither for nor against the pause; he was only very skeptical about it. What encouraged its promoters was a hint from the Russians that if the U.S. agreed to a serious pause, lasting at least twelve days, it could lead to serious negotiations. The Russians did not guarantee anything, but they said, "We'll try," and, "We think there is hope." They said they made a serious effort to persuade Hanoi to enter into talks, and if the North Vietnamese had done so, they could in effect have had the pause extended for nothing; but they didn't.

The President hesitated about the pause for a long time. He was at his ranch in Texas and kept his own counsel. Only at the last minute did he agree not to resume bombing after the thirty hours' Christmas truce ended on December 26. But he rejected what was called the "soft option"—to link the pause with an offer of negotiations—and adopted instead the "hard option," without the offer. There was no bite from Hanoi.

Johnson's decision to send high-ranking emissaries to various capitals on December 29, 1965, ostentatiously sounding out the prospects for a negotiated settlement, looked to some like too much of a propaganda effort; but in most capitals it was taken seriously. Averell Harriman, for instance, impressed the Polish Government with his exposition of the President's intentions to such a degree that it decided to send its Under Secretary of the Foreign Office, J. Michalowski, to Hanoi. Johnson at least for a time persuaded the world that he was not the bellicose man it had assumed, and that he wanted peace. There was still no response from Hanoi; on the contrary, its official newspaper, *Nhan Dang*, sounded a tough note.

At the same time, however, the newspaper criticized certain dissident elements in Hanoi's own ruling group. It is now known that the North Vietnamese Politburo had met on December 18, shortly before the pause, and looking back now some of the experts wonder if an earlier pause could have affected some of the decisions taken at that meeting. It was evident from the article that some Politburo members must have argued in favor of negotiations, but had been overruled. An earlier pause might have strengthened Hanoi's doves; but by the time it began, the decisions had already been made, decisions which must have meant an escalation by North Vietnam.

The pause did produce a faint reaction in Rangoon, the only capital at the time where both North Vietnam and the United States maintained embassies; but the response came six hours after bombing had been resumed, and to the State Department it did not look like a serious feeler.

The pause lasted thirty-seven days in addition to the initial truce and was Mr. Johnson's most important overt move for peace so far. An important chance was missed, probably because Hanoi was in too defiant a mood. The hope that silence would speak louder than explosions was badly shattered. President Johnson never quite forgave those who pressed for the pause. He believed he had been taken for a sucker, that he had lost forty days (in all) of softening up the enemy. Dean Rusk was not surprised that it led nowhere; he believed there was no prospect for negotiations until the U.S. could decisively alter the military balance of power in its favor.

While the pause went on, a Soviet mission, led by Alexander Shelepin of the Central Committee, visited Hanoi on January 7 to arrange for increased military aid to North Vietnam.

American public concern about the war grew perceptively as television began to carry its ugliness more and more frequently and more and more vividly into every living room. In Congress opposition to the war became increasingly vocal. The President's determination increased likewise; in common with many Americans, he was infused with the firm belief that the military can achieve anything, and that in the end the situation was bound to improve.

Already he saw ample signs that the situation in the field was improving. He had a desperate need to believe that it was, and the optimistic outlook of Walt Rostow, whom he brought back to the White House in March,

1966 (replacing McGeorge Bundy as his Adviser on National Security Affairs), helped him to do so.

What would have happened to the Vietnam policy if a little conspiracy had succeeded and Walt Rostow had failed to get the White House job leaves one today only with a tantalizing afterthought. But a conspiracy existed at that time, not so much against Rostow as in favor of slipping Bill Moyers, the President's Special Assistant and former Press Secretary, into the chair left vacant by McGeorge Bundy's departure. Moyers was very anxious to get a policy-making job. When George Ball left the under-secretaryship of the State Department, for instance, Moyers made it obvious to the President that he wanted that job; the President didn't listen. Now after McGeorge Bundy's departure another great opportunity opened up, but Moyers had little hope that the President would offer him the job, and so he tried to take matters into his own hands. He and Francis Bator, a deputy to McGeorge Bundy, quietly decided to assume together responsibility for the National Security Council staff. They had an inkling that Jack Valenti was urging President Johnson to put Walt Rostow into that job, and neither Moyers nor Bator was enamored of the idea. To bring matters to a head, Moyers and Bator decided to call the National Security Council staff together to stage a kind of take-over. The meeting was set for noon and the Council was within ten minutes of convening when the President announced the appointment of Walt Rostow. Was it a coincidence? No one knows. But the President did know that Moyers and Bator were doveish, and since he still believed that he could win the war, he selected the strongest possible hawk for the job.

For a long time Mr. Johnson had hoped that, by speaking about it as little as possible, he could keep Vietnam and the creeping escalation of the war out of the American conscience; but his secretiveness began to backfire. He had avoided a great debate the previous August (after he had decided on the sweeping escalation in July) and this had seriously undermined Congress's trust in him. Some of his aides now believe that in early 1966, after the bombing pause, he missed a golden opportunity to explain his policy, to test the country's support for the war, and to cement public opinion. But I doubt whether he could have had any lasting effect. After the pause many world leaders (notably the Japanese) viewed the American position with far greater sympathy, but at home the restlessness about this undeclared war began to rise. So too did the pressures for more escalation.

At a dinner party on January 13, 1966, the late John McNaughton, Assistant Secretary for International Security Affairs at the Pentagon, told me of a conversation with General Earle Wheeler, Chairman of the Joint Chiefs of Staff, the previous August. Wheeler had then said that victory was the U.S. aim, and therefore he had decided on pouring more men into Vietnam. But now, McNaughton told me, Wheeler was using a different argument: he was saying that unless more men were sent, more American soldiers would be killed. Wheeler had assured him, though, that with enough men he would have the enemy beaten into submission by the end of 1966. McNaughton foresaw that more troops would have to be sent to Vietnam, and he held out little hope for de-escalation. He saw no indication that the other side was willing to signal anything. Peace feelers, he said, were "like making smoke signals in a high wind."

In February McNamara still thought there was a finite number of troops that the North Vietnamese could infiltrate into the South, and that once that level was reached they would either attempt to negotiate or let the war die down. He also liked to catalogue the enormous increase in American firepower. John Kenneth Galbraith, the Harvard professor, discussing McNamara at a dinner party, said, "He is an organization man who, once a decision is taken, accepts and supports it. He does not fight, as some Cabinet members do, a guerrilla war within the Administration."

On February 19 Senator Robert Kennedy advocated the inclusion of the National Liberation Front in any post-war Saigon government, and two days later Vice-President Humphrey criticized him for saying so. On March 2 Secretary McNamara announced that U.S. forces in South Vietnam had reached a total of 215,000 men, and another 20,000 were on their way there. Almost at the same time Australia declared its intention of tripling its Vietnam contingent from 1,500 to 4,500 by June, 1966 (both Australian and New Zealand statesmen later admitted that they contributed troops to the Vietnam War not because of the importance they attached to the war itself, but so as to have the U.S. in their debt in case they themselves for some reason stood one day in need of American help).

In May, McNamara predicted a further increase in U.S. troop strength in order to offset rising North Vietnamese infiltration. But he also delivered a wide-ranging, almost philosophical speech of which the basic theme was that even the greatest arsenal is no substitute for policy, that military power can only be supplementary to diplomatic, economic, and political ingenuity and initiative. In a reference to internal violence, he said that "the local people themselves are best able to deal directly with the situation within the framework of their own traditions." The speech reflected his first doubts about the war. He sensed not only that it looked endless, but also that it was having a profound effect on the unity of the United States without the promise of creating a strong political base in Saigon.

Yet, as McNamara's hesitations grew, the President became even more convinced of the need to intensify the war. Late in June, before giving the Air Force permission to bomb oil depots and military targets within the suburbs of Hanoi, the President asked for the support of Prime Minister Harold Wilson. Up till then Wilson had loyally supported Mr. Johnson despite the dissatisfaction it caused within the Labour Party. Wilson had already warned the President that he would be unable to go along with such an escalation as was now proposed, and now refused to do so, dissociating the British Government from the American decision. Since there was no going just halfway with Mr. Johnson, Wilson ceased to be the kind of loyal ally whom he could trust.

The night American bombs for the first time ignited oil storage depots in the Hanoi and Haiphong areas, President Johnson seemed almost scared of himself. He stayed up until the first reports about the raids were in. As he waited in the loneliness of the White House, afraid that something might go wrong, his daughter Luci entered with her fiancé, Pat Nugent. She quickly realized her father's psychological state and suggested that he go to her church to pray.

The President ordered his car and drove to the empty church at around 11 P.M. There he kneeled on the hard floor and prayed. Luci's priest came, talked to him, and comforted him.

On his return to the White House the reports were reassuring. The targets were hit as planned and no bombs went astray—none had hit Soviet ships, as the President said he feared, or a populated area. When Luci went to his room late that morning and heard of the raids' success, she said, "See what my little monks can do for you."

Johnson used to tell this story to many visitors, perhaps to indicate how much of a conscience he had, how much he himself suffered by the decisions he had to take. That night became known as "the night of the little monks."

The raids improved President Johnson's immediate position and that of the Democratic Party by having made it clear that he was now pursuing military victory. Tom Wicker, the *New York Times* columnist, concluded that as a consequence the Democrats would enter the 1966 congressional elections with the immediate advantage of a policy of strong action; but he added, prophetically, "If the promised success does not become apparent, the President might well be called to account later—perhaps in 1968."

This was a period when the President waited expectantly for the enemy to "cry uncle." It was also the time when the estrangement between him and Robert McNamara began to set in. Hanoi did not "cry uncle," and the Russians indicated that Hanoi had no intention of coming to the conference table; Hanoi had made plain, apparently, that it would not consider negotiations while the bombing went on. The Russians were not certain that the North Vietnamese would negotiate even if the bombing stopped. If Hanoi were destroyed, they thought, North Vietnam would retreat to the jungle rather than give up or talk.

The Russians seemed certain that China would not send any troops, but thought the Chinese might offer some of their airfields should those in North Vietnam be destroyed. One thing the Russians also made clear was that they would have to increase their own aid, especially for antiaircraft defense.

Both Russians and Americans misread each other's intentions in Vietnam. The Russians began to say around Washington that they had misjudged Mr. Johnson, that instead of being another Franklin D. Roosevelt (one of their heroes) he was nothing but a Texas Truman. American calculations partially went wrong because they underestimated the support the Russians would finally give to the North Vietnamese.

But while the Russians were saying that Hanoi was in no mood to consider negotiations, the Poles had sent out a highly secret peace feeler. Like another later, conducted in London, it is worth examining in detail for the light it sheds on the hesitations, mischances, and complexities of the attempts to find a path to peace.

IV

Marigold:

The Stunted Peace Flower

The Americans usually code-named Vietnam peace feelers after flowers—though there was an Indian one that was called Nirvana—and the Polish initiative of 1966 became known as Marigold.

Janusz Lewandowski was his country's representative on the International Control Commission, a last remnant of the old Geneva agreement that still twitched like the sundered tail of a lizard. The Commission's airline remained a sort of shadowy link between Hanoi and the outside world, and its members flew regularly between the North and Saigon, maintaining contact even though they had nothing official to transmit.

In June, 1966, however, with the help of the Italian Ambassador to South Vietnam, Giovanni d'Orlandi, Lewandowski began to meet with U.S. Ambassador Henry Cabot Lodge in Saigon. Though for a time nothing much seemed to happen, the meetings went on, for Lodge believed that the North Vietnamese situation had deteriorated to a point where a real desire for negotiations might be developing in Hanoi. More American troops were being sent to Vietnam; the bombing of the North was being intensified; and the President's resolution to fight to the bitter end was evidently firmer than ever.

Marigold began to flower on November 14, when d'Orlandi, in whom Lewandowski's confidence reposed, told him that Lodge would like to see him again. According to another version, it was Lewandowski who said that he wanted to see Lodge before flying to Hanoi the following day. Whoever took the initiative, the two met on November 14, and Lodge told Lewandowski that the U.S. was interested in an approach to Hanoi. Next day, after instructions from Washington, Lodge presented Lewandowski with a number of specific suggestions. Chief among them was, in an elementary form, what later became a highly technical and complex proposal (the "Phase A-Phase B" plan) offering a deal for mutual de-escalation—a halt to U.S. bombing in return for an end to North Vietnamese infiltration of the South. As Lewandowski understood the proposal, however, the stopping of the bombing did not depend on any prior promises or commitments by Hanoi. Lodge also outlined American thinking about the ultimate settlement of the war.

Lewandowski left for Hanoi as he had planned. Meanwhile, the Polish Foreign Minister, Mr. Rapacki, and his Under Secretary, Mr. Michalowski, had gone to Sofia for a meeting of Communist leaders, and there took the opportunity to tell both Mr. Brezhnev, Chairman of the Communist Party of the Soviet Union, and the North Vietnamese Foreign Minister, Nguyen Duy Trinh, what Lewandowski was doing. Brezhnev said he hoped the Poles would continue their efforts, and promised Russian support.

Lodge's proposals were transmitted to Pham Van Dong, the North Vietnamese Prime Minister, by Lewandowski on November 20, though not until November 25 were they able to talk directly. By then Lewandowski had condensed Lodge's proposals to ten points; they apparently differed from what Lodge had said in language, but not in substance.

Pham Van Dong was skeptical; after all, Lewandowski had only spoken from notes, he had nothing official. Lewandowski explained that the U.S. would stop the bombing if there could be an assurance that after a certain time negotiations would begin on the ten points. This was a more generous offer than any subsequently made, because it involved U.S. willingness to stop bombing before the other side made a reciprocal move. The ten points included such questions as the future neutrality of South Vietnam, its national sovereignty, and the question of self-determination; most important, they made clear that the U.S. was ready to discuss with representatives of the "parties fighting in Vietnam" constructive proposals for bringing the war to an end.

All this was considerably more explicit than the fourteen points that Harriman and the other peace envoys had disseminated around the world on their peace campaign the previous January. Then there had been no doubt that Hanoi was not prepared to negotiate; the U.S. had had only 100,000 men in Vietnam, and the members of the North Vietnamese Government had not believed that she might send as many as 500,000; Hanoi had been still convinced that it would win the war; and the Chinese had put on maximum pressure to prevent any possibility of Hanoi's negotiating in the wake of the bombing pause.

Now, at the end of the year, the North Vietnamese seemed to the Poles to begin to doubt their prospect of an early victory, and instead they saw ahead of them the likelihood of a long and costly war. Moreover, Chinese influence was said to be less pervasive.

This seemed plausible, for on December 28, Pham Van Dong asked Lewandowski not to quote him directly but to let the Americans know that if "the U.S. was ready to confirm what he understood were the views expressed in conversation between Lewandowski and Ambassador Lodge, the North Vietnamese Embassy in Warsaw would be instructed to get in touch with the U.S. representative in Warsaw." The North Vietnamese, he added, wanted to find out whether the U.S. was sincere and whether the ten points could be considered a basis for negotiations.

Lewandowski flew back to Saigon and met Lodge on November 30 and December 1, telling him the ten points he had used to summarize the American position, and passing on the message.

On the next two days American bombers, which had not been flying missions because of the monsoon, took off in large numbers to attack targets outside Hanoi. Bombs fell in an area between five and forty miles from the capital.

On the second day of these raids, December 3, Lodge told Lewandowski that the American Ambassador in Warsaw had been instructed to be ready to meet a representative of Hanoi after December 6. Lodge also confirmed that the views he had expressed broadly represented the U.S. position, although certain points were subject to "important differences of interpretation."

When Foreign Minister Rapacki and Mr. Michalowski met the American Ambassador to Warsaw, Mr. Gronouski, in Warsaw on December 5, they asked what these reservations implied; Gronouski said he did not know. They also raised the question of the bombing, asked what it meant in relation to the forthcoming talks, and warned that it could raise doubts in Hanoi about the sincerity of the U.S. approach to the talks.

On December 7 the North Vietnamese Ambassador in Warsaw told the Polish Foreign Office that Hanoi also felt concern about the bombing and was reviewing the situation. At that point he was still uncertain whether, if there were talks, he would represent Hanoi or whether a special representative would be sent; he had, however, been instructed to meet Gronouski, though he was to await further guidance as to the substance of their discussions.

Two days later Ambassador Gronouski was able to inform Rapacki that the resumption of bombing had been a straightforward military decision based on the reappearance of good weather after an interval of several weeks. But when on December 13 some bombs hit the inner city of Hanoi during another, badly led bombing raid, a message reached the Polish Government from Hanoi that the negotiations had been canceled.

There were further talks, however, between the Poles and Gronouski on December 19 and 20, and on December 21 Gronouski went to Washington. He returned to Warsaw three days later, and, although the Poles begin celebrating Christmas with their traditional Christmas Eve dinner, Rapacki instead met Gronouski. He brought with him from Washington a gesture of "good will"—the U.S. would ensure that no bombs would fall within a radius of ten miles around Hanoi. This proposal originated with John McNaughton after a talk with a Russian official. The Poles passed it on to Hanoi, but on December 31 the North Vietnamese reply made it plain that they no longer believed in American "good will," and therefore were unwilling to continue the negotiations.

Those few in the Johnson Administration who knew about Marigold were skeptical of Polish intentions and uncertain of the validity of Lewandowski's efforts; they wondered whether this young foreign service officer might merely be an "eager beaver" trying to prove himself. As to the Polish Government's position, Mr. Rusk remembered Mr. Gromyko's remark to him at the U.N. General Assembly to the effect that the U.S. should not pay too much attention to the various attempts by Eastern European diplomats to act as interlocutors between Washington and Hanoi; only Russian initiatives really mattered. However, later in January a Russian official in Washington confirmed the genuineness of the Polish initiative.

American suspicion was also aroused by the way that Polish officials in their talks with Gronouski reacted critically both to the bombings on December 2 and 3 and to Washington's reservations about Lewandowski's ten points (which could have been interpreted as nothing more than diplomatic caution; the Poles however, suspected that the U.S. had had second thoughts about the proposals offered by Lodge).

Among those American officials actually involved in the maneuvers I found sharp disagreement as to whether or not one of those precious opportunities for a way to peace had been lost; all, however, had some uneasiness of conscience, because the bombing had provided the enemy with the perfect excuse for withdrawal. Some have tried to excuse the action as one of those left-hand-right-hand errors of coordination. Some blamed a blanket authority issued by the President to the military to bomb whenever the weather permitted, and claimed that it was impossible for this to be countermanded at very short notice. Several high officials, however, have since confessed that the bombing was not due to error or oversight but was carried out on a decision by the President; perhaps, they say, a very determined effort to reverse his decision could have delayed the action, but with Mr. Johnson at his Texas ranch and very little time in which to put on the pressure, it would have been a long shot indeed. Another high American official later remarked: "Everything the President did in November and December, 1966, went wrong. Maybe his gall bladder operation at the time is to blame."

After his retirement, Dean Rusk privately expressed his regret about the inept handling of Marigold; apart from this, however, the only satisfaction for the Poles was a blessing from the Pope after the Italian Ambassador, Signor d'Orlandi, told him about the initiative. It was the first time that the Pope and the Polish Government exchanged such notes.

When the Poles later related details of the operation and its failure to U Thant, and their account leaked to the press, it engendered Mr. Johnson's monumental ire.

Disconcertingly for those who try to arrive at the true history of such affairs, the Americans also now like to compare the Polish initiative with one made much later (in January, 1968) by the Rumanians. The difference, it is said, is that while the Rumanians provided exact reports about their exchanges with the North Vietnamese, Washington was never quite certain exactly what messages were passed and what replies received between the Poles and Hanoi.

In January, 1967, the Johnson Administration went through one of its periodic waves of optimism. Ambassador Lodge even went on record as predicting "sensational" military gains during the year. He also doubted that open peace negotiations would ever take place; he thought the war would in some way peter out.

On January 28, the North Vietnamese Foreign Minister asserted in an interview with the Australian correspondent Wilfred Burchett that it was only after an unconditional ending of the bombing and other acts of war that "there can be talks between the two countries." The State Department saw no change in Hanoi's position in this statement. At the same time, the American chargé d'affaires in Moscow was instructed to get in touch with the chargé d'affaires of the North Vietnamese Embassy to deliver several important messages for Hanoi.

One was to confirm plans for the bombing pause during the Tet holiday; another was to make clear that a partial cutback in the bombing was a deliberate move. The third was to have special significance for Prime Minister Harold Wilson, who was shortly to entertain Premier Kosygin in London.

V

Harold Wilson:
The Penalties of Distrust

Harold Wilson had great expectations of Premier Kosygin's visit to London in February, 1967. He hoped it would provide an opportunity for him to step onto the world stage as a mediator between the Americans and the North Vietnamese. He had known Kosygin for years, and felt he had something of a special personal rapport with him.

There seemed also to be new straws in the wind. On January 3 the North Vietnamese Premier, Pham Van Dong, asserted that Hanoi's four points were not "conditions" for peace talks but constituted a "basis for settlement" and "valid conclusions for discussion." Two days later the North Vietnamese chief diplomatic representative in Europe stated that if the U.S. would "definitely and unconditionally" stop bombing his country, Hanoi would "examine and study" proposals for negotiations. Some discounted these straws as nothing but straws; others wondered whether they were not hints of a slight shift in Hanoi's position.

In Washington, President Johnson was tired of volunteer mediators; and ever since Mr. Wilson had dissociated himself from the bombing of oil installations near Hanoi, seven months earlier, the President had ceased to consider him a robust ally. Wilson's self-appointed mission with Kosygin only aggravated the mistrust. Yet it was difficult for Johnson to say no to Harold Wilson; it would have been very awkward if it had become known that the U.S. would not try out such a special opportunity for peacemaking.

The chosen liaison man was Chester Cooper, a short, bushy-browed, slightly Chaplinesque member of Ambassador Averell Harriman's staff. He had "low visibility": he would not be spotted by the press. Thanks to his dry humor and his easy ways with the British, he had been well liked in London ever since his CIA days between ten and twelve years earlier. He had the subtle mind needed for this task—yet, as it proved, he did not quite have the support and influence in the White House necessary to the challenge that developed.

Cooper had in fact just visited London, early in January, to brief the Prime Minister and George Brown, the Foreign Secretary, about the fruitless Marigold feeler. Wilson had been annoyed at not being informed of it sooner. Brown had been infuriated: on a visit to Moscow the previous November he had transmitted the so-called "Phase A-Phase B" proposal for gradual scaling down of the war by both sides (a proposal which was to play so pivotal a part in the events of the next few days), and now he had learned from Cooper that he had not been the only one to do so. The fact that the Americans were not sure that the proposal had actually reached Hanoi via Warsaw was no real comfort.

Shortly before Kosygin's arrival, Harold Wilson asked Secretary of State Dean Rusk if Cooper could return to bring him fully up to date on the American negotiating position. Rusk agreed and Cooper flew back to London on February 3. He was instructed to hold nothing back from the Prime Minister, and to provide a channel of communication with Washington.

Before he set out, Cooper had seen three drafts of a letter from Johnson to Ho Chi Minh, along the lines of the Phase A-Phase B proposal. Phase A provided that, under a prior secret agreement, the U.S. would stop the bombing of North Vietnam "unconditionally." Phase B (1) provided that the North Vietnamese would stop the infiltration of men into the South, and Phase B (2) that the U.S., as a corollary, would refrain from sending any further troops to Vietnam. The U.S. would agree to the first part of the proposal only if Phase B (1) was also accepted in advance. The key to the proposal was the time-lag between Phase A and Phase B; this was vaguely a "reasonable period," understood to be from about ten days to no more than two weeks, in which Hanoi would determine that bombing had stopped under Phase A and not simply for some technical reason or because of weather conditions.

The President hesitated about sending this letter to

Ho. It was a difficult decision; he had never before taken such an initiative. What Cooper did *not* know when he left for London was that a letter had been sent on January 7—but it was an uncompromising one, quite different from the drafts that he had seen. In it the President said that he would be "prepared to order a cessation of bombing against your country and the stopping of further augmentation of U.S. forces in South Vietnam as soon as I am assured that infiltration into South Vietnam by land and sea has stopped." In other words, in contrast to the Phase A-Phase B proposal, the President was now prepared to act only *after* being assured that infiltration had stopped.

The letter was delivered by the American chargé d'affaires in Moscow to the North Vietnamese mission there on February 8. The idea, according to some, was to preempt the Wilson-Kosygin talks and to forestall the possibility (which the State Department suspected might be a probability) that Wilson would sign his name to Hanoi's latest formula: this, as put by North Vietnam's Foreign Minister on January 28, was that there *could* be talks after the unconditional ending of the bombing. Others suggest a simpler motive: if there were to be negotiations, Johnson wanted to be the one to conduct them.

The Prime Minister's hopes for the Kosygin meeting were high; George Brown's were less so. Wilson's hopes sank when the Russians announced their delegation: it did not include Foreign Minister Gromyko or a known Asian expert, and it looked more like a good-will than a business visit.

Undaunted, Wilson asked the American Ambassador in London, David Bruce, if Cooper could stay on for the duration of the Russian visit. The White House skeptically agreed; it suspected Wilson's motives and did not want to encourage him. In addition, Walt Rostow considered Cooper a dove and therefore an untrustworthy emissary. At the State Department, however, there was a feeling that perhaps Wilson could bring something off and, anyway, there was little to lose in trying.

Kosygin arrived on Monday, February 6, on the eve of the cease-fire in Vietnam over the Tet holidays; this gave special meaning to the timing of the visit. Wilson met him at the airport. As they rode into London, Kosygin said that he wanted to discuss international problems, including Vietnam. Wilson was greatly encouraged.

Next day, when the talks began, he put forward the ingenious Phase A-Phase B proposal. Kosygin at first countered by saying that the interview given by Hanoi's Foreign Minister to Wilfred Burchett was a genuine attempt by Hanoi to get negotiations started, and that it represented a major concession. He also indicated that talks could begin from three to four weeks after the bombing halt. In a speech at Guildhall, much to everyone's surprise, Kosygin mentioned the reconvening of the 1954 Geneva Conference, of which Britain and Russia were co-chairmen.

Contrary to Washington's expectations, Harold Wilson loyally insisted that the Phase A-Phase B proposal was the best approach to negotiation. He paid no attention to the mention of the Geneva Conference, and Kosygin did not repeat it. Wilson held his position until finally, on Friday, Kosygin said, "You keep telling me about this two-phased proposal—put it into writing." The proposal seemed new to him, though it was what (in a simpler form) George Brown had given to Mr. Gromyko when they had met the previous November.

For the first time the Russians were showing a real interest in getting involved in backstage peacemaking. Kosygin, according to the Prime Minister, had also told him explicitly that he was in touch with Hanoi, that he thought Hanoi was in a receptive mood, and that he was worried that if nothing happened the Chinese would again be able to assert their influence on the North Vietnamese.

After lunch on Friday, Chester Cooper and Donald Murray, Asian expert in the British Foreign Office, sat down together and drafted a short memorandum. Around 4 P.M. Cooper sent the text to Washington, confident of immediate approval. After all, it was within the fairly loose instructions with which he had left Washington. The memo did, however, contain a sentence to the effect that nothing would be done until a reply was received. So sure was he of Washington's approval that when by 7 P.M. no reply had been received he decided to go to the theater to see *Fiddler on the Roof.*

Harold Wilson was equally confident that the memo conformed to the American position; it had been drafted by Cooper, the special emissary, and he had discussed the whole matter with Ambassador Bruce almost every evening of the week. He put his copy of the memo in his pocket and went to the Soviet Embassy to attend an early evening reception in honor of Mr. Kosygin. At an appropriate moment he handed the draft proposal to the Russian, who, according to the Prime Minister, seemed confident that it might open the way to progress. When later that evening Wilson met Bruce and Cooper, both were hopeful that the cause was advancing.

At least, they were until 10:30 P.M. Then Walt Rostow called Wilson direct on the "hot line" from Washington and told him, brusquely, that the terms originally presented were no longer on offer. Wilson was ordered, in no uncertain terms, to inform Kosygin of this forthwith.

What most perturbed the Johnson Administration at this point was that increasingly heavy supplies were reported to be moving south and that enemy troop concentrations had been spotted poised along the Demilitarized Zone. So that when the Cooper draft arrived in the Situations Room at the White House, it aroused grave misgivings.

Wilson twice during the week had been asked by the President (through Cooper) to tell Kosygin that the increased infiltrations violated the current Tet truce, and should be stopped immediately, and Wilson had done so.

The substitute formula that was now flashed over the teletype machine from Washington to Downing Street had more the quality of an ultimatum than an offer to negotiate. A time interval between Phase A and Phase B had become unacceptable to the President; infiltration had to stop *before* he would halt the bombing.

Walt Rostow, McNamara, even the President sat up that night redrafting the memo. Rostow was insensitive to the theme; McNamara was inexperienced in diplomatic drafting; and the President, who focused for the first time on the intricate language of the proposal, was quite appalled by the concession to Hanoi that it entailed. At the same time no one in the White House realized quite what they were doing to Harold Wilson's credibility with Kosygin.

Hopping mad with embarrassment, Wilson had to send his private secretary that night to catch Mr. Kosygin before his train left Euston Station for Scotland, and hand him the new message. Kosygin never returned to the Phase A-Phase B proposal again.

Later, at about 11 P.M., Wilson got on to the President over the "hot line." Johnson repeated that his offer had been withdrawn. The Prime Minister complained bitterly about this abrupt *volte-face,* and the "hot line" began to run at a higher temperature than usual. The only explanation Wilson could see for this reversal, which had badly undermined his credibility with Kosygin, was that either he had not been kept properly informed or the hawks had won the upper hand, or somebody on the American side didn't know his ass from his elbow. In reply the President put all the emphasis on the gross breaches of the truce and the heavy movement of supplies south, which he and the Joint Chiefs of Staff thought endangered the security of American troops.

Walt Rostow's accusation that Wilson should have delayed handing the original memorandum to Kosygin until it had been cleared in Washington only made the Prime Minister angrier, for he had every reason to believe that it represented the American position. Hadn't Cooper and Bruce, who both knew what it was all about and neither of whom could be called a fool, seen all the cables? It was not surprising that he had assumed Washington's approval of Cooper's message to be only a formality. (Cooper, too, became the target of Washington's ire, and was threatened with dismissal until it was found that he had not exceeded his instructions.)

Undaunted by this embarrassing setback, Wilson decided nonetheless to put forward a new proposal; it would be quite different but it would still get the President's approval. He would put it to Kosygin on his own responsibility. It was to bring the crisis between London and Washington to an angry climax.

Wilson's new proposal was an attempt to extend the current bombing pause beyond the Tet truce, conditional on Hanoi's agreeing to halt infiltration immediately. On Sunday morning it was transmitted to the President. Both Wilson and Cooper wanted to make quite sure this time that they had Johnson's approval before they informed Kosygin.

In Washington, as he met his advisers to decide how to reply, Johnson was in one of his worst moods. He was annoyed by the whole Wilson attempt to negotiate with Kosygin, and he suspected him of having done so more in his own political interests than in Johnson's. Nor did he like negotiations by proxy, for they somehow put his own good faith into question. He complained that he always had too many volunteer intermediaries and negotiators. At one point he asked rhetorically: "If you knew Harold Wilson's outlook, would you want him to negotiate for you?" He did not want to be trapped into another "goddam pause," and snapped at those who pleaded for the extension by saying, for instance, to Nick Katzenbach, the Under Secretary of State: "Nick or someone else is going to tell me . . . but I'm not buying any of that"; or "Bob McNamara got so involved in that thirty-seven-day pause and here he's going again. I wish I had not followed his advice for the first time . . ."

But some of those present had the impression that

they were debating a decision the President had already made. Johnson always became angry if he felt that he had to act on some peace feeler on a ten-to-one chance, and always felt that he was being "conned" into something. He usually agreed to take the chance, but it took him also to the limits of his patience.

Cooper, meanwhile, had been installed in a hideout on the second floor at Chequers, the Prime Minister's country house, in a room once used as a prison. Sir Burke Trend, the Secretary of the Cabinet, kept him company. Cooper had a direct telephone link with the White House. Down below, Wilson and Kosygin began their last meeting. Brown, who in the previous three days had offered his resignation about four times, was not present. Soon it was getting late, and there was still no word of Washington's willingness to extend the bombing pause on the basis Wilson had proposed. Dinner was being served especially slowly, and Mr. Wilson sat there, secretly nursing his proposal, spinning out conversation about the Common Market and what it might mean to the Soviet Union.

Upstairs Cooper was getting impatient. He had promised Wilson an early reply, and Walt Rostow (who had been rude and impatient) became contrite and repeatedly promised one as soon as possible. By 10:45 P.M., when nothing new had come through, Cooper called the White House again. Still no decision. Cooper called yet again, and got Rostow on the line.

But downstairs they had long passed the coffee stage.

Kosygin was ready to leave and Wilson could stall no longer. As he said goodbye he told Kosygin that he might have a message for him from the President, and suggested that it would be better if he did not go to bed immediately on arrival at Claridge's. The police escort revved up their motorcycles and Cooper, in utter desperation, leaned from the window and held out the telephone receiver as far as he could so that Rostow, across the Atlantic, could gain a proper sense of urgency from the sputtering noise of the departing outriders.

Finally, at 11:00 P.M., Cooper was told that the President had agreed to delay the bombing resumption; the message was being drafted and would be awaiting Wilson on his return to 10 Downing Street. At 12:15 A.M. Wilson, Bruce, and Cooper met there to read it and to decide what to do. Not only the Prime Minister but also Ambassador Bruce had tried hard to obtain an extension of the bombing pause. Bruce, who is one of the most patient of men, lost his temper several times in talking to the intemperate and at times rude (at least to him) Rostow over the transatlantic telephone. Officially the Tet truce had ended some hours earlier, and the fact that the bombing had not yet been resumed meant that an unofficial extension was already in progress. Johnson's message now confirmed an official extension until 10:00 Monday morning, London time. That gave just enough time for Kosygin to leave London before bombing was resumed; he was due to depart at 9:30. Johnson, remembering how offended the Russians had been when he ordered the bombing of North Vietnam while Kosygin was in Hanoi, decided to avoid offending both Russian and British prime ministers similarly.

As an extension it was disappointingly little, but Wilson decided to tell Kosygin of it, nevertheless. He and George Brown went to Claridge's at 1:00 A.M., armed this time with the message signed, for authentication, by Ambassador Bruce and written on the stationery of the U.S. Embassy. Wilson wanted insurance against another misunderstanding with Washington.

The Russian leader's reaction to that after-midnight meeting was not encouraging. He interpreted the message as coming close to an ultimatum. Seven hours for Hanoi to reply, he felt, was too little. He would pass the message on, but he did not think it would be acceptable. It simply did not leave enough time.

Wilson offered to try for a further extension if Kosygin on his part would press Hanoi for an early reply, and left Claridge's at 2 A.M. By the time he returned, after a few hours' sleep, to accompany the Russian visitor to Gatwick Airport, he was able to inform him that Washington had agreed to another five hours. Kosygin sounded depressed. He thought this still did not leave enough time for a reply, and predicted that Hanoi would turn the offer down, especially since it could not afford to withhold completely all supplies from its forces in South Vietnam.

Kosygin took off from Gatwick, there was no further word from him, and bombing was resumed. The peace initiative had collapsed—not only for Wilson, but also for Kosygin. There is indeed some reason to believe that Wilson's last message, though forwarded by Kosygin for transmission to Ho Chi Minh, was in fact never sent on from Moscow. His colleagues must have decided that he had not done well enough, and that it could only create embarrassment.

To most of those involved in all the various peace feelers, this seems in retrospect one of the most significant because of the Russian willingness to become involved in mediating, or to be a transmission agent between the U.S. and North Vietnam. But why it was treated by the Johnson Administration with such lack of sympathy I have not been able to establish with certainty, even though I have talked with most of the principals involved. It is not clear whether American thinking was dominated by mistrust of Wilson and a decision to prevent his becoming an important cog in the peacemaking machinery, or by the feeling that it was an inopportune moment to enter into negotiations.

Off and on, the U.S. had tried hard to interest the Russians in a mediating role, but they had steadfastly refused and simply repeated Hanoi's position, which was that a complete and unconditional halt in the bombing would lead to negotiations. But Johnson was too soured by the failure of the thirty-seven-day pause to listen to that; he did not want to make a significant commitment.

The Russians had their problems. There was clearly a great difference between their ignoring Fidel Castro and taking their own missiles out of Cuba, and what sway they could exercise over the North Vietnamese. Not only was their influence with Ho Chi Minh limited, but the Chinese, too, had their supporters in Hanoi's Politburo. The Russians let it be known in Washington that they had only limited scope for maneuver, and were facing several dilemmas. They did not want to promise the Americans anything they were not sure they could deliver; nor did they want to give the impression that they were trying to force something down North Vietnamese throats or that they were letting down a Communist ally. They knew that the Chinese were waiting for the chance to jump on them with propaganda accusing them of betraying the Communist cause.

They were also confused, just as Hanoi probably was, by the credibility gap that Johnson created for himself with the policies that he advocated during the 1964 election and afterward. In the beginning the Kremlin probably accepted that he wanted to carry on in the Kennedy tradition. But as his position in Vietnam hardened, as he escalated the war, they came increasingly to mistrust him. They could not be sure whether, if they succeeded in getting negotiations started, Johnson would not demand terms so unacceptable to Hanoi that the terms would become an embarrassment to them. They were therefore very chary of helping Johnson, who (they suspected) wanted to attain at the conference table the victory he had failed to win on the battlefield.

Moreover, they were more than annoyed that he ordered the first bombing of North Vietnam when Mr. Kosygin was visiting Hanoi. That in itself must have led the Kremlin to abandon any mediating efforts it might have been considering at that time.

The Russians seemed worried, at least in the beginning, that the war could lead to a confrontation between them and the United States. As the North Vietnamese continued to hold their own, and as they refused direct military aid from both the Chinese and the Russians, the Kremlin became less interested in mediation and probably found some pleasure in seeing the American Goliath pinned down and embarrassed by the North Vietnamese David.

Gradually, as more Soviet arms were sent to Hanoi and as the Chinese not only cut down their own aid but tried to impede the flow of Russian supplies, Moscow's influence in Hanoi began to grow. This fact, and the rising cost of Russian aid, may have persuaded Mr. Kosygin to his London overtures. When, on arrival, he actually broached the subject, this was news. And how ever much American mistrust of Mr. Wilson there was, there is no doubt about the significance of Kosygin's request that the Phase A-Phase B proposal be put into writing. The Russians are not in the habit of taking such initiatives without good reason; they act only when they think it will lead somewhere.

President Johnson did not take this sufficiently into consideration, either because he did not want to negotiate at that point, or because he still felt he could win a limited victory on the battlefield. He also seemed overwhelmed by the reports that the North Vietnamese were exploiting the truce to resupply their people in the South.

Chester Cooper did his level best to advise the Prime Minister and to put pressure on the White House, but he clearly could not carry enough influence. Rostow distrusted him, and that meant that the President distrusted him, too.

Mr. Johnson's distrust of Mr. Wilson may have been an even greater handicap. He was afraid that the Prime Minister, in his eagerness to play the peacemaker (or, as Mr. Rusk once put it, his hope of getting the Nobel Peace Prize), would give away some of the carefully hoarded presidential chips. Mr. Johnson was not a man to let anybody else play with his chips.

Mr. Wilson became a victim of his own good intentions and his ambitions as a peacemaker; and a victim, too, of his own misjudgment of Johnson's prejudices against him. He was rewarded with some uncharacteristically shabby treatment by the Americans. The episode had a tragic effect on Anglo-American relations. A chance to test the Russians in Vietnam peacemaking was lost—and now no one will ever know how real a chance it was.

VI

The Last Illusions of Victory

The U.S. restarted the bombing and Hanoi Radio sounded as tough as ever, stubbornly reiterating North Vietnam's demand that the bombing had to be halted "unconditionally and for good." The ten-mile circle around Hanoi was observed for a while, but after April 16 it was disregarded. Both sides hardened their positions. Hanoi's disclosure of correspondence between President Johnson and Ho Chi Minh only underlined the irreconcilable hostility. In the key paragraphs of his letter Johnson wrote:

> There is one good way to overcome this problem and to move forward in the search for a peaceful settlement. That is for us to arrange for direct talks between trusted representatives in a secure setting and away from the glare of publicity. Such talks should not be used as a propaganda exercise but should be a serious effort to find a workable and mutually acceptable solution.
>
> In the past two weeks, I have noted public statements by representatives of your Government suggesting that you would be prepared to enter into direct bilateral talks with representatives of the U.S. Government, pro-

vided that we ceased "unconditionally" and permanently our bombing operations against your country and all military operations against it. In the last day, serious and responsible parties have assured us indirectly that this is in fact your proposal.

Let me frankly state that I see two great difficulties with this proposal. In view of your public position, such action on our part would inevitably produce worldwide speculation that discussions were under way and would impair the privacy and secrecy of those discussions. Secondly, there would inevitably be grave concern on our part whether your Government would make use of such action by us to improve its military position.

With these problems in mind, I am prepared to move even further towards an ending of hostilities than your Government has proposed in either public statements or through private diplomatic channels. I am prepared to order a cessation of bombing against your country and the stopping of further augmentation of U.S. forces in South Vietnam as soon as I am assured that infiltration into South Vietnam by land and by sea has stopped. These acts of restraint on both sides would, I believe, make it possible for us to conduct serious and private discussions leading towards an early peace.

Ho Chi Minh in his reply simply repeated his well-known position:

It is only after the unconditional cessation of the U.S. bombing raids and all other acts of war against the Democratic Republic of Vietnam that the Democratic Republic of Vietnam and the United States could enter into talks and discuss questions concerning the two sides.

The prospects for peace seemed gloomier than they had for a long time; no reasonable basis for negotiations was in sight. In private Mr. Johnson sounded more determined than ever to increase military pressure. The Gallup Poll showed that 67% of the American people were in favor of bombing North Vietnam and Johnson's own popularity rating was down to 62%, but the division among Americans over the war had become more bitter, more emotional.

A meeting between Johnson and President Ky of South Vietnam in Guam on March 20 only added to the confusion. At the start President Johnson set a guardedly optimistic tone. He defined the moment as "a favorable turning point, militarily and politically," but after the meeting was over he said, "We have a difficult, a serious, long-drawn-out, agonizing problem that we do not yet have an answer for." His generals told him that they had seriously sapped the enemy's strength, yet the battles had become more rather than less intense. For the time being, at least, the emphasis was on intensifying the war generally and the bombing of the North in particular (though the mining of Haiphong Harbor was still being resisted by Mr. McNamara).

On March 28, U Thant disclosed that his proposal for a standstill truce as a first step toward peace negotiations had been approved by the U.S. and South Vietnam but rejected by Hanoi. By June, according to official figures, U.S. troop strength in South Vietnam was 463,000; combat deaths stood at 11,099 and the number of wounded at 67,083. South Vietnam had 600,000 men under arms and had lost 47,695 dead.

In the following month two Frenchmen with direct access to Ho Chi Minh went to Hanoi. Their names were Raymond Aubrac and Professor Herbert Marcovich, and the man who claims credit for having arranged their visas is the Australian correspondent, Wilfred Burchett, whose credentials were highly acceptable in Hanoi. He cabled the North Vietnamese Minister of Health from Pnompenh, where he was then based, explaining that the two Frenchmen wanted to establish contact between the Pasteur Institutes in France and in North Vietnam. He apparently did not know that the pair were actually on a highly secret diplomatic mission to sound out the prospects for negotiations.

Aubrac, a director of the United Nations Food and Agriculture Organization, came to know Ho Chi Minh in his Paris days, and they had become good personal friends. Marcovich, a microbiologist at the University of Paris, had met Dr. Henry Kissinger of Harvard (now President Nixon's Adviser on National Security Affairs) at one of the Pugwash meetings organized by Cyrus Eaton, the Cleveland rail magnate, to promote contacts between Western and Eastern European scientists. It was through Marcovich that Kissinger met Aubrac, and the Harvard professor acted as intermediary between the two Frenchmen and the Johnson Administration.

Kissinger had been to Vietnam himself several times, at least once on a mission for Ambassador Lodge.

He went out a moderate hawk and came back, having talked to province chiefs, feeling that politically the South Vietnamese Government was hardly viable, that its writ in the country hardly counted. Having already acted as consultant for three Presidents—Eisenhower, Kennedy, and Johnson—Kissinger was experienced in carrying out special missions and in addition had the advantage that, as a private person, he could easily be disowned should things go awry.

This new operation lasted several months, and was one of the few feelers to lead to negotiations of a sort, a kind of give-and-take between Washington and Hanoi. After the first contact Kissinger debriefed the two Frenchmen and gave President Johnson a mildly optimistic report. The State Department decided to keep the channel open, but when it asked the two to revisit Hanoi they failed to get new visas. Instead they were told to report to the North Vietnamese representative in Paris. At one point Chester Cooper (that self-effacing "fiddler on the roof" at Chequers earlier in the year) went to Paris to offer proof to the two Frenchmen and the North Vietnamese that Kissinger spoke with the authority of the American Government—though, indeed, Kissinger's part in the operation was conducted in the most professional manner. The exchanges continued until October and were abandoned only when Hanoi let the channel dry up.

They included, however, some important hints of new positions on both sides. For the first time the North

Vietnamese said *pourrons* ("will be able") instead of *pourrions* ("would be able") to express their definite willingness to negotiate if the U.S. halted the bombing. Officials closely connected with the operation are still reluctant to admit that this strong hint was conveyed to them at the time; they prefer to maintain that Hanoi continued its refusal to commit itself to negotiations, and that there was no modification of its attitude until December 29, 1967, when Nguyen Duy Trinh issued a statement to the effect that "after the U.S. has ended unconditionally the bombing and all other acts of war against the Democratic Republic of Vietnam, the DVR will hold talks with the U.S. on questions concerned." (In an interview with the *Agence France Presse* on February 8, 1968, Trinh reemphasized that "the talks will begin as soon as the U.S. has proved that it has really stopped unconditionally the bombings and all other acts of war against the DVR.")

But the hint was there in the operations via Kissinger nonetheless, and it led to a great deal of dissent in Washington as to how far the Administration should empower Kissinger to bring about actual negotiations. Some maintain in retrospect that if the U.S. had been willing to make the kind of concession that President Johnson offered later—the partial bombing halt which he proposed in his "abdication" speech of March 31, 1968—negotiations might have begun sooner than they in fact did.

Nevertheless, on its side the U.S. made a greater concession than ever before in authorizing Kissinger to transmit to Hanoi what later became known as the "San Antonio formula" (named after the city in Texas where President Johnson offered it as a basis for negotiations in a speech on September 29, 1967). In relative terms this formula was a considerable step forward, for until then the President had given the impression that he did not believe in negotiations that involved concessions on his part; in agreeing to various negotiating formulae he would make concessions to his critics in his own Administration, but not to the enemy.

Dean Rusk time and again repeated that the bombing of the North would stop as soon as the North Vietnamese left their southern neighbor alone, and that if Hanoi would like to do this by agreement, then the U.S. would be glad to sign. Anything beyond this Rusk considered undesirable or unacceptable. But enough pressure for something new came from Robert McNamara to make Paul Warnke, then the new Assistant Secretary for International Security Affairs in the Pentagon, jot down with a member of his staff (on his return from the Kissinger debriefing) a new formula. McNamara liked the new idea. It did away with any preconditions for stopping the bombing and was based on the simple assumption that Hanoi would not take advantage of a halt. McNamara took Warnke's draft to the President, and Mr. Johnson accepted it, most likely without fully comprehending its meaning. The State

Department never quite accepted it; Dean Rusk continued to insist on assurances from Hanoi first.

When the President announced the formula in San Antonio, the public did not know that Ho Chi Minh had already failed to accept it during the Kissinger-guided exchanges early in September. Later, because of the feeling in Washington that Ho had misunderstood the formula, as he had not seemed to see anything new in it, another effort was made to clarify its subtlety, but after this last effort via the Kissinger channel nothing more was heard from Hanoi.

In his speech, the President said: "Our desire to negotiate peace . . . has been made very, very clear to Hanoi, directly and many times through third parties. As we have told Hanoi time and again, the heart of the matter is really this: the U.S. is willing to stop all aerial and naval bombardment of North Vietnam when this will lead promptly to productive discussions. We, of course, assume that while discussions proceed, North Vietnam would not take advantage of the bombing cessation or limitation."

Here was a definite departure from the President's tough proposal in his February letter to Ho, which demanded a halt of all infiltration before a bombing pause. Now the North Vietnamese would be allowed to continue infiltration, even after the bombing halt, *at the existing level.* It clearly indicated to Hanoi that the U.S. was saying, in effect, "We'll stop bombing, but for God's sake don't embarrass us by stepping up your infiltration rate." To a certain degree, the condition was a mere formality, because, first, it was always difficult to estimate the infiltration rate, and, second, according to CIA estimates, the bombing never seriously interfered with infiltration anyway. Nevertheless, there was a change in the U.S. position, and one that Hanoi had been aware of since the Kissinger moves.

The full emphasis of the President's cryptic concession, however, did not receive public attention until four months later, when the *New York Times* followed up a dispatch of mine to the *Sunday Times* in London with an editorial that said (on January 31, 1968):

> There have been indications . . . that in private contacts with Hanoi, Washington's position may not have been so inflexible as it appeared in public. It has been reported in the *Sunday Times* of London that the President privately is no longer insisting on some form of de-escalation by North Vietnam. The British newspaper's Washington Correspondent, Henry Brandon, says that the phrase "not take advantage of a bombing halt" does not require the North Vietnamese to reduce their military infiltration but only that they not increase the level of men and supplies flowing into the South. In return, the U.S. reportedly has indicated a willingness not to send reinforcements of its own to South Vietnam.

Some leading Administration spokesmen, notably Mr. Rusk, had given the speech a public interpretation to the effect that it represented no change in the American position. The official admission that a major concession by the U.S. was inherent in the San Antonio formula had to wait until the confirmation hearings held for Mr. Clark Clifford on Capitol Hill on March 3, 1968, two days after he had succeeded Mr. McNamara as Secretary of Defense. Walt Rostow then made it abundantly clear, in private conversation, that he disapproved of Mr. Clifford's revelation (which was, of course, a revelation for the American public but by no means for Hanoi).

When, before its christening, the San Antonio formula was put to Hanoi in the Kissinger exchanges, it marked a turning point, for it must have helped to impress on at least some members of the North Vietnamese Politburo that the U.S. was offering more than equitable terms for talks.

By midsummer, 1967, the approved U.S. troop ceiling of 480,000 men had been reached, and the President was considering requests for more. In early August the new maximum was 525,000. The war meanwhile had become an unpopular cause, and because of it Mr. Johnson had become the most unpopular President since the Second World War. And yet, paradoxically, it was Vietnam that accounted for most of the strength he still had in the country. The doves were more vocal, but the hawks remained strong if inarticulate. It was the hesitant people in the middle whose numbers were increasing.

In October, Townsend Hoopes, Under Secretary of

the Air Force, followed up two earlier studies McNamara had ordered in spring and early summer, and produced a fifteen-page document pulling together all the difficulties in the way of a military victory. It asked whether there was an ultimate ceiling to the number of men America could put in, and how the Chinese would react if this number reached one million. It laid out the growing threat to the dollar caused by the loss of gold, and it analyzed the increasing criticism of world opinion. The paper reflected the growing sense in the Administration that the U.S. was doing nothing in Vietnam but reinforcing weakness.

By then McNamara had gone publicly on record before the Senate Armed Services Preparedness Subcommittee with the view that the war could not be won by bombing the North, but only on the ground in the South. He stated firmly his opposition to widening the range of bombing targets in the North, and declared that no level of bombing or direct air strikes on population centers (which the U.S. considered immoral tactics) would help win the war. What he said reflected the conclusion contained in the Hoopes memorandum and three other reports that McNamara had ordered: a monthly one from the CIA, one from the Joint Chiefs of Staff, and one by a group of experts outside the Government. The majority view was that air bombardment had never seriously impeded the flow of supplies, that the enemy in the South never suffered serious shortages because of the bombing, and that in a year's time the situation would not be much different. This sharply contradicted Walt Rostow's view, in which bombing the North was the key to victory. Air Force assessments, on the other hand, focused on how the U.S. could do better. And the objective always was how to make the enemy pay a higher price.

Gradually, as the war had widened, so the frustrations had mounted, and the original purpose of preventing infiltration came to be changed to "bomb them to the conference table." This increasingly visceral reaction also became President Johnson's. McNamara's public denigration of the bombing of the North outraged the President. It led not only to an acrimonious scene between the two, but also to Johnson's losing confidence in his Secretary of Defense's judgment in regard to the war in Vietnam. From then on, McNamara's influence waned rapidly.

The advocates of air power were always bullish about what could be accomplished. They consistently claimed more than could be achieved. North Vietnam was not an industrial area, like Germany in the Second World War; it lacked vital targets, and the damage that could be done from the air was limited. Operational Air Force officers, of course, consider themselves a "can do" outfit, and so will never admit that they cannot accomplish what is asked of them. Yet it would be wrong to assume that the Air Force is a monolith; it, too, reflects a spectrum of opinion. In Vietnam the Air Force did the job it was asked to do with remarkable fidelity to the

very stringent ground rules. It held to the specially pre-
scribed approaches to certain targets, for instance, although they were often the most dangerous approaches;
and those who did not carry out orders faithfully—as,
for example, the pilot who dropped his bombs close to a
Russian ship in Haiphong Harbor—were severely pe-
nalized. The usual reply to critics of the ineffectiveness
of air warfare maintained, as the Senate Military Preparedness Committee did, that the Air Force was
shackled, and if only it could bomb Haiphong Harbor
it would have an effect on the war.

The Committee's scathing criticism of McNamara
aroused to his defense his fellow rationalist McGeorge
Bundy, who had by then left the White House to become President of the Ford Foundation. He too had
grown doubtful of the effectiveness of military measures,
however well executed, in a limited war. In a letter to
the *Washington Post* he took the Subcommittee to task:
"Nothing is less reliable than the unsupported opinion
of men who are urging the value of their own chosen
instrument—in this case military force. We must not
be surprised, and still less persuaded, when generals
and admirals recommend additional military action—
what do we expect them to recommend?" He warned
that careful judgment was required to distinguish
military value and political costs. While the ideologists
continued to hold fast, the rationalists had had second thoughts: as McGeorge Bundy now confessed,
"Gray is the color of truth."

The Last Illusions of Victory

Since I am concentrating here on the battles fought out in the recesses of government in Washington, and not those in the rice paddies of Vietnam, I am including here only a few relevant conclusions I reached on my last visit to South Vietnam in October, 1967; they are taken from a dispatch to the *Sunday Times* in London on October 15:

> Looking back over my three crowded weeks here, what has struck me most is the difference between what is called the "time frame" needed, as seen by the military, and the frame of mind of American public opinion. Unless there is a closer relationship between the two, unless military strategy is reviewed in the light of the American mood at home, it is not likely to succeed, however unpalatable this may be from a purely military point of view. The United States is the prisoner of its earlier optimism. Not only has it undermined credibility at home, but probably also in Hanoi.
>
> Next, I believe that the military situation is now manageable for the United States with the resources allocated. Her forces cannot be dislodged, nor could the North Vietnamese score a Dien Bien Phu kind of knock-out blow.
>
> At the same time, it seems to me that there is no military solution to this war. There is some bitter truth in the image of the tiger being unable to catch the mosquito; it can only be done by homemade Vietnamese flypaper.
>
> For too long, the Americans have allowed the South Vietnamese to assume that they will carry them on their broad shoulders to victory. So much so that the belief developed that this is an American not a Viet-

namese war. Ambassador Bunker has been trying to correct this belief, but the resistance to mobilization, as expressed to me by President Thieu, continues. . . .

Taking all this into account, the war, except at the Demilitarized Zone where the North Vietnamese continued to press their advantages, could be played in a lower key. It would further reduce its pace and its cost in money and men.

This might steady the growing dissension among American public opinion. For it is steadiness that will be necessary, especially if it comes to frustrating, long-drawn-out negotiations with Hanoi. And if negotiations prove impossible then steadiness will be even more important.

As regards American political strategy, it would be useful if the United States redefined its limited political aims in Vietnam. Much has happened since the Manila Declaration. The American effort here is staggering. But it has also given the South Vietnamese an inferiority complex and made them adopt a let's-leave-it-to-the-Americans attitude. They see it as an American war, not their own. . . .

Pruning rather than escalating the war would add credibility to limited American aims and also to American willingness to see this war through how ever long it may take. This, of course, is easier said than done, especially since many Americans believe that victory is eluding the United States because President Johnson is resisting further escalation. But the crux of the President's problem is to make American strategy reflect the long-term, not the short-term, outlook of this contest.

Withdrawal would have dire psychological repercussions throughout Asia, and further escalation is unlikely to force the enemy into negotiations. A low-pressure war, on the other hand, might be more tolerable for American public opinion, might impress Hanoi, and might promote prospects for negotiations, even though at present these prospects are not good.

Washington would like to give the new government in Saigon another three to six months to establish itself, and Hanoi seems to want to await the course of the American election campaign. North Vietnamese spokesmen have said that once the battle becomes "indecisive," the simultaneous fighting and negotiating period begins.

The trouble with this peculiar war is that neither side knows who is ahead, but it is an old axiom that indecisive situations usually produce peace settlements that are more lasting.

Just before Christmas, 1967, General Westmoreland, the U.S. Commander in Vietnam, and Ellsworth Bunker, the Ambassador in Saigon, returned to the U.S. to sprinkle some optimism into everybody's ears. They talked about "light at the end of the tunnel," but many suspected that Johnson was using them to set the right mood and tone for the presidential election year of 1968.

The McNamaras then gave a dinner party in honor of Ambassador Bunker and his charming wife, the Ambassador to Nepal, Carol Laise. The President and Mrs. Johnson came, and the President exuded charm and humor and affection for his hosts throughout the evening. The latter, therefore, were more than a little surprised when a few days later McNamara was informed that the President had cleared his way to the Directorship of the World Bank.

Public pressure was mounting for the President to end the bombing of North Vietnam to test Hanoi, but he had come to relish being embattled—or (and this is perhaps truer) he had become determined to make the best of a bad situation. In his State of the Union message he was no longer the Great Society crusader but a man on the defensive, forced to retrench. For a President who wanted so much to better the world, an ebullient Texan who believed that he could remake the U.S., win a war and, like Atlas, carry the world on his shoulders, this was an unhappy stance, one that did not come easily.

In his disenchantment he sought refuge and solace in seeing himself as the lonely, brave President who must endure the bitterness of his countrymen, who would "meet the trials these times impose" as did Abraham Lincoln, Woodrow Wilson, or Harry S. Truman. He now preferred to be right rather than popular, and this engendered in him a new self-confidence—not that all-conquering Texan cockiness, but of a ruminative and philosophical kind. Unlike the Russians, who know when and how to retreat if necessary, Americans (and especially President Johnson) favor a heroic interpretation of history. Johnson felt reinforced by the failure of any potential Republican candidate to come up with better alternative policies. He still seemed more afraid of the hawks than of the doves, and he was probably correct in thinking that the cement of nationalism and patriotism was holding together a narrow majority of Americans in support of his war strategy.

More and more people, however, came to realize that the war had reached a stalemate. That word was resented in the Johnson Administration, but until the Tet offensive in February, 1968, its use was accurate. The Tet offensive, which penetrated to the U.S. Embassy in Saigon, caught the American forces off guard and showed how vulnerable they still were, but the American counteroffensive, so to speak, restored the stalemate. It did not, however, restore the lost confidence in the political and military assessments from Saigon. It unnerved some of the most seasoned hawks. And it marked the beginning of a fundamental change in the appraisal of the war from Washington.

What added to the shock was what is generally referred to as General Westmoreland's request for 206,000 troops. This "request" had exactly the opposite effect from what was intended. It reinforced the wave of pressure under which the Johnson Administration was reeling, and it raised such monumental questions that it proved in the end to have a devastating effect on the men around President Johnson, and finally on the President himself. It proved also to have a traumatic effect on General Westmoreland.

VII

Revolt of the Elders

Dean Acheson, once Truman's Secretary of State, was an old and trusted friend of President Johnson, with a similar outlook on the war. In February, 1968, before leaving for a holiday in Antigua, Acheson was given an optimistic briefing: almost immediately the bloody Tet battle shattered the optimism. He began to feel that the war was going to lose the election for Johnson, that the country was going to the dogs—and that the President was getting one-sided information. On his return he went to the President and told him so.

To Mr. Acheson's suspicions that the President was not getting all the war information he should, Mr. Johnson's reply was an invitation to talk to his advisers himself. Acheson demurred, saying that this would not do: he would only get the same stuff the President was getting. Could he instead have authority to talk to anyone in the Administration? The President readily agreed.

Acheson found his suspicions confirmed: the President *was* getting a one-sided picture. He and the President lunched alone, and he told Mr. Johnson this. He also implored him to believe that it did not make sense to carry on stubbornly on his present course, especially in view of General Westmoreland's latest request for massive troop reinforcements. Westmoreland reminded him, he said, of the obstinate Civil War general McClellan, who had gone on and on, hoping for victory, however long it might take. But for Mr. Johnson time was running out. The war was ruining him and ruining the country and couldn't be won in the foreseeable future. It seemed to Acheson that even a million men wouldn't make enough difference. These were surprising views from him. The President was deeply shaken, and said so.

For most people that "light at the end of the tunnel" of which General Westmoreland had spoken so confidently on his last visit to Washington suddenly seemed very distant; for some, it was even extinguished. The enemy's ability to contest the control of almost every city and town in South Vietnam had come as a complete surprise. It brought home with a vengeance how fragile and vulnerable was the edifice that the United States had built there. A sense of humiliation swept down Pennsylvania Avenue, all the way from the White House to the Capitol, and only gradually did this change into a grim determination that was reflected in the drawn, fatigued faces of the highest policymakers.

It was true, as President Johnson said, that he had had "detailed information on Ho Chi Minh's order governing the offensive." But General Westmoreland had prepared the President only for a big offensive against the outpost of Khe Sanh and for minor diversionary attacks in its vicinity. Westmoreland had badly underestimated the enemy's capabilities elsewhere, and had so concentrated his forces to protect Khe Sanh that he had weakened the cities' defenses; and the enemy had taken full advantage.

In spite of the anger and frustration in Congress, greater restraint prevailed than one might have expected. As one Congressman put it: "We are getting over our illusion of omnipotence."

On February 4 I had a long private interview with the President. Its main purpose, it seemed to me later, was to convince me how wrong everybody was who believed that the Tet offensive was a success for the enemy. Johnson got angry and bitter when talking about the general tendency to interpret the offensive as an American setback. "When they lose 10,000 men and we 400, is that a setback? Is that losing?" he exclaimed. "When we get 5,000 of their men as prisoners—is that losing? When they fail to achieve an uprising in the cities, is this victory? It's easy to stage these raids against the cities and to attack the U.S. Embassy, but what did they get out of it? Nineteen men got into the Embassy compound and not one got out again. Twelve times some men succeeded in getting across the fence around the White House here in Washington but that does not mean that they won a victory." Raising his voice further, "If we had attacked cities and civilians the way the

North Vietnamese have done, just imagine how the American press would have reprimanded us. But when Ho does it, nobody complains, and nobody says that military victory eluded him. If you were President you'd get sick of reading the *New York Times*."

It was therefore of great comfort to him that General Westmoreland had assured him that within a month the U.S. would be much further along than it was possible to see then. And as to the battle of Khe Sanh, whose defense was seen by many as a grave mistake, he said that he received unanimous advice to make a stand there. He said the story in a magazine that he asked the Joint Chiefs of Staff to give him this in writing was wrong, but that he had consulted every general he respected, including Ike and General Ridgway.

It was a heartbreaking period for the President. Victory suddenly looked remoter than ever. There was a mood of desperation between the lines of what he said to me that day, but it only seemed to reinforce his determination to win that "coonskin."

Further shocks were in store for the President, however. Another old reliable hawk was about to fly off the perch. On March 1, 1968, Clark Clifford took over from Robert McNamara as Secretary of Defense. An intimate friend of the President, and by profession a lawyer, Mr. Clifford had always accepted the premise that the U.S. had interests and commitments in Southeast Asia. He had always shared the deep concern about Communist expansion in the area, and he was also convinced that if the U.S. had not sent out troops in force, South Vietnam would have been lost to the enemy. As the President's friend and counselor, he therefore often reinforced Mr. Johnson's conviction of the need to prosecute the war.

In the late summer of 1967—when he was still a private citizen, and practicing law in Washington—he had gone with General Maxwell Taylor on a mission for the President to all the so-called troop-contributing countries in the Pacific area: Thailand, Australia, New Zealand, Korea, and the Philippines. He returned from this tour with a sense of uneasiness, even dismay. He had come to the conclusion that these allies did not agree with the American analysis of the importance of the war, the basic premises of which he had accepted— that the U.S. had to persevere in Vietnam because of the danger of Communist expansion, because the future of all Southeast Asia and the Western Pacific was at stake, and because the United States' own national security was involved. The allies felt no urgency, no real sense of danger, certainly nothing to compare with their feelings when Japan had been on the march in the Second World War. In addition, the increased troop contributions that the President had managed to obtain from them had been minimal.

Still, the Press was readily able to identify Clifford as a hawk when he moved into the Pentagon, because it was known that he had opposed the thirty-seven-day bombing pause promoted by Mr. McNamara in December, 1965 (Mr. Clifford felt strongly at the time that it was the wrong signal to give to Hanoi, because the U.S. asked nothing in return). He assumed his duties as Secretary of Defense amidst the shock and confusion that followed the vicious Tet offensive. He had hardly been sworn in when he was asked by the President to preside over the examination of General Westmoreland's latest request—206,000 additional troops.

What made this policy review so important was that it became the education of the new Secretary of Defense and made him the most impassioned opponent of the war. His doubts about its wisdom had been slowly building up; he came to the conclusion that he had to apply all the influence at his command to prevent a further escalation. How he finally changed his mind, how he risked forfeiting his long friendship with Mr. Johnson, and how he helped to force the South Vietnamese Government to the negotiating table in Paris without Presidential approval is perhaps the most dramatic story of this unhappy war.

The request that began the review had its origin on February 3, when General Earle C. Wheeler, Chairman of the Joint Chiefs of Staff, reported to General Westmoreland a conversation with a "senior authority" during which he was requested to ask Westmoreland "if there is any reinforcement or help we can give you." Five days later there was a more direct message from Wheeler to Westmoreland, asking him: "Do you need reinforcements? . . . We can provide the Eighty-second

Airborne Division and about half of a Marine Corps division." On February 12, General Westmoreland replied to the effect that "there be deployed immediately a Marine regiment and a brigade package of the Eighty-second Division and that the remaining elements of those two divisions be prepared to follow at a later time."

Just three weeks later, General Wheeler flew to Saigon on orders from the President to find out what else General Westmoreland wanted. Westmoreland presented him with an "outline reinforcement plan" developed by MACV (Military Advisory Command Vietnam) and based on the assumption that the President would agree to call up the reserves. It listed in detail all the units to be requested and their deployment, including sailing dates, stretching over a year. It added up to 206,000 men. The Joint Chiefs of Staff, who processed the request, clearly felt that the psychological situation after the shock of the Tet offensive was ripe for the calling-up of reserves on a large scale, something that President Johnson had resisted time and again, with the result that the U.S. armed forces were badly overstretched.

"I never dreamed of being accused of having asked for 206,000 men," General Westmoreland said a year later with a mixture of bitterness and resentment. He is a proud man, and understandably it was hard for him to stomach the implication of the request—that he had suffered a major defeat in the war—especially in view of the fact that he subsequently was successful in restoring something of a stalemate in the military situation.

Westmoreland claims first of all that it was not he who generated the "request," but that it came from Washington after consultations between the President and General Wheeler. The two asked him how many troops he needed, first of all to restore the U.S. position after Tet, and next to win the war. Secondly, Westmoreland says that the plan was prepared in the light of what was needed under the prevailing uncertainties at the time. The questions asked were: What were the North Vietnamese intentions and capabilities in the northern areas? Would the South Vietnamese Army hold firm? Would the North Vietnamese launch another offensive? Would the situation after the *Pueblo* incident (the capture by the North Koreans of a U.S. reconnaissance ship) calm down or get worse? His request, therefore, was nothing more than a prudent estimate of what would be needed over the next twelve months, especially in the light of CIA estimates which assumed that the enemy could commit more fresh troops than MACV's intelligence estimates allowed for.

Westmoreland also insists that during the debate about the "request" inside the Administration he was never consulted either about its overall wisdom or its details. What shocked him most of all was that his request with the exact figure of 206,000 was "leaked" to the *New York Times*, and once it had become public knowledge, it created outside psychological pressures that affected the men on whom responsibility for the decision rested.

There was another aspect of the affair that troubled Westmoreland, that seemed almost to gnaw at his conscience: the fact that because of this request, and all it implied, everything became unstuck—the President took the decision to offer Hanoi a partial bombing halt that led to the Paris negotiations which Westmoreland, bent on military victory, had not foreseen, and he would have preferred that they not take place.

However tortuous these afterthoughts may be, the General finds comfort in the conviction that the President's withdrawal from the elections had nothing to do with the military situation in Vietnam. He recalls the President mentioning in November, 1967, that he had decided to withdraw from the race. (Mr. Johnson had spoken vaguely in these terms for some time, but none of those who heard it took him too seriously. When I heard of his having said it to several members of the Cabinet in January, 1968, I, too, discounted it. When I mentioned, though, to one of the President's closest friends on April 2 how annoyed I was with myself for not having written about it in January, he comforted me by saying, "None of us were certain until the President announced his decision on March 31.") What General Westmoreland remembers is that the President in November said to him that he had already *decided* to withdraw and had then asked how Westmoreland thought this would affect the war and the political situation in Saigon.

Contrary to General Westmoreland's recollection of the origins of the request, the civilian policymakers all agree that they interpreted it (and it had by that time become a request from the Joint Chiefs of Staff) as a firm demand for that many more troops; and they express surprise at the General's claim that the plan was only a contingency request to be stretched flexibly over twelve months. The fact remains, they insist, that it required an immediate critical decision whether or not to recommend to the President a mobilization of the reserves—that was the crux of his request, and that was why it caused so extensive a reappraisal.

The men engaged in the review over which Mr. Clifford was asked to preside were Mr. Rusk, Walt Rostow, Generals Wheeler and Taylor, Richard Helms (Director of the CIA), William Bundy (Assistant Secretary for Far Eastern Affairs), Paul Nitze (Deputy Secretary of Defense), and Nicholas Katzenbach (Under Secretary of State). After a week's intensive study, the President's advisers were ready to go far in meeting his request. Their initial recommendation, though, carried no signatures and no date.

But in the course of the study Mr. Clifford's extraordinary and fateful transformation took hold. Gradually a deeper and deeper conviction gripped him that the United States could not win a military victory under the restrictions laid down by the President. The major restrictions were that the North would not be invaded, Haiphong Harbor was not to be mined, and the enemy was not to be pursued into Laos and Cambodia. Mr. Clifford, it should be noted, fully agreed with these restrictions.

The men who greatly influenced his thinking were Paul Warnke, Philip Goulding (his Assistant Secretary for Public Affairs), and Paul Nitze—in about that order. He also discovered that there were a good many others harboring doveish ideas, such as David E. McGiffert, Charles F. Baird, and Townsend Hoopes (Secretaries of the Army, Navy, and Air Force respectively); Alain Enthoven, in charge of Systems Analysis; and, among the younger civilians, Dr. Morton Halperin, Richard Steadman, and Les Gelb.

The Joint Chiefs' pressure, which Clifford resisted, was for 100,000 men within a few months and the rest later—but all by June, 1969. Only the full number, they insisted, would lead to victory. Rusk, as usual, kept his own counsel. Rostow, with something closer to bemusement than his usual passion, backed the JCS. Helms (as was his habit) took no personal side but let the facts of his CIA reports speak for themselves, and they supported neither the military assessments nor an optimistic view of the prospects for victory.

The debate continued for another two weeks, but no matter how persuasively Clifford argued—and he is a brilliant lawyer—he failed to persuade the others to see the situation his way. And equally no one could persuade him that more troops would resolve the war (see his article in *Foreign Affairs*, July 1969); he was convinced they would only mean more fighting, more casualties, higher costs, and a more deeply divided United States. Neither Clifford nor the other side would surrender. The argument became a war within a war, and personal bitterness grew.

President Johnson was deeply upset by Mr. Clifford's resistance to the majority view, which he himself seemed to share. During this period the President delivered two emotional speeches in which he summoned up the shadow of Britain's Neville Chamberlain to warn Americans against appeasement, and he exhorted the nation that it should, if necessary, "win peace on the battlefield." None of his speeches during that month was sent in advance to Clifford's office, as they had been previously.

This did not mean, however, that the President was unaware of growing doubts about the war among others whom he trusted. For instance, Senator Richard Russell, the Georgia Democrat who was Chairman of the Senate Armed Services Committee, made critical remarks about General Westmoreland, and even as devoted a member of the "Congressional-military complex" as Senator John Stennis, from Mississippi, had great reservations about mobilizing the reserves. "Joe" Fowler, the Secretary of the Treasury, was brought into the discussions, and he warned of the danger of a heavier gold drain; at one point during March, when European banks suddenly refused to cash American traveler's checks, the President realized how close to the edge of a precipice the dollar had come.

In his distress, Mr. Johnson turned to ex-President Eisenhower, who had always sustained him in the determination to pursue the war to victory, and during a speaking tour he stopped at Palm Springs, California, just to consult him. He asked the general how long a President should back a military commander. Eisenhower replied that a President must back his general as long as he had confidence in him—if he lost this confidence, he should replace him. He also stressed that Westmoreland had a much more difficult task in Vietnam than he had had in Europe in the Second World War with five and a half million soldiers. He had always known where the enemy and the front line were; in Vietnam, said Eisenhower, you never knew where the enemy was and there was no front line. He went on to praise General Westmoreland as an outstanding commander.

President Johnson, recalling this conversation a few days later, reaffirmed his own confidence in General Westmoreland's abilities. Ten days afterward, however, he announced Westmoreland's replacement by General Creighton Abrams and his promotion to Army Chief of Staff. It is true that this switch had been talked about for some time; many people had in fact expected it to happen earlier. The question why the President chose this particular moment offers numerous possibilities for speculation. Was it because he was about to decide on a different military strategy? Was it because his confidence in the General, in spite of what he was saying in private, was not what it had been? Or was it simply as good a moment as any to relieve General Westmoreland of one of the most taxing commands any military man might hold, and one in which he had already remained longer than he should?

Anyone who had the opportunity of seeing President Johnson around March 11, 1968, in person and in private, was taken aback by the near-exhaustion that had overcome him. He was a man in torment as I had never seen one before. His face was ashen, his eyes sunken, his skin flabby, and yet, underneath, his expression was taut.

"We are the flies that captured the flypaper," James Reston had written in the *New York Times* in February, a few weeks earlier. "We are stuck with our concept of a military victory." The great debate in the White House, as it continued to seesaw, was about whether and how to get unstuck.

"It was a lonely, stultifying, miserable period," Mr. Clifford confided to a friend. But he was to receive some help from unexpected quarters, when the President agreed to call together what used to be referred to as his Council of Elder Statesmen. They had not met since the autumn of 1967 when, after an optimistic report by

General Westmoreland, they had reached the unanimous view that American policy was heading in the right direction.

Now they foregathered in Washington once more on March 25. They included Dean Acheson; George Ball; General Omar N. Bradley, retired Second World War commander; McGeorge Bundy; Arthur H. Dean, President Eisenhower's Korean War negotiator; Douglas Dillon, Secretary of the Treasury under Kennedy; Associate Justice Abe Fortas of the Supreme Court; Arthur Goldberg, U.S. Ambassador to the United Nations; Henry Cabot Lodge, twice Ambassador to Saigon; John McCloy, U.S. High Commissioner in West Germany under President Truman; Robert D. Murphy, a veteran diplomat of the Truman-Eisenhower period; General Matthew B. Ridgway, retired Korean War commander; General Maxwell Taylor; and Cyrus R. Vance, former Deputy Secretary of Defense and President Johnson's troubleshooter.

They first dined with Dean Rusk as their host. Afterward they adjourned to the briefing room where they were briefed by the CIA's Vietnam expert George Carver; by the State Department's experienced Vietnam hand, Philip C. Habib; and by Lt. General William DePuy of the Pentagon, who had served on General Westmoreland's staff in Vietnam. The briefings were surprisingly candid and depressing. George Carver especially gave a discouraging evaluation of the impact of the Tet offensive. Neither Habib nor DePuy exuded optimism. The discussion continued late into the night.

Next morning the group met again in the White House, and this time Rusk, Rostow, and Clifford were present. Clifford made it clear that he had no intention of supporting the request of the Joint Chiefs of Staff. In his view their sights had to be brought down, and he would agree to sending only nominal reinforcements.

Then the senior statesmen had lunch with the President. Dean Acheson, who sat next to Mr. Johnson, offered to lead off the discussion, and Johnson agreed. Acheson warned him that what he was going to say might cause pandemonium, but again the President encouraged him. Acheson then summed up his impressions of the discouraging briefings they had had, the heavy military losses, the damage to the Saigon Government's authority, and the disarray in the pacification program.

To Acheson's surprise, his views were shared by more among those present than he had expected. The one who mattered most, because he too had been a strong supporter of the war, was McGeorge Bundy. He summed up for those supporting Acheson's views and admitted, in self-flagellating mood, that "for the first time in my life I find myself agreeing on this issue with George Ball."

General Wheeler, Chairman of the Joint Chiefs, was unconvincing in his presentation of his own views and in his inability to define his objectives in the war. (He later pointedly asked what sort of a "jerk" had briefed the "wise men." Some of them thereafter worried about the briefers' future.)

When the President was asked what *his* objectives were, he was not very persuasive either. He simply repeated what he had already enunciated in public speeches.

Acheson said that bombing was of no real importance (he had not believed in its efficacy for some time). It would serve neither to make the North Vietnamese give in, nor even to make them state what they would offer in exchange for a halt. Sooner or later, they would make their own concessions, without spelling them out in advance. Acheson concluded that the American objective should be to maintain the Saigon Government at the lowest possible cost to the U.S., and that the U.S. should start withdrawing men, at least the "Coca-cola pushers"; this would not weaken the front lines. Ball, Goldberg, and to a lesser degree Vance, but above all Mc-George Bundy, were on his side. Only Justice Fortas, General Taylor, and Murphy stood firm in advocating the hard line.

The lunch upset the President. "Who poisoned the well?" he asked complainingly. But the poison now began to circulate in his own bloodstream, too. The man who resented "bitchers and moaners," who always believed that serious emergencies had to be met by men of guts (Churchill was his preeminent example), and that "good men will be strong in the face of aggression," was in a deep quandary. He believed in Rusk and Rostow, both men absolutely loyal to him. Rostow had helped him greatly; not only was he a tireless adviser, but he showed a tender, human, supportive feeling for the President that was of great comfort and consolation; he often reminded the President that Lincoln, too, had suffered gnawing agony. On the other hand there were Clifford, Acheson, and McGeorge Bundy, all formidable men and once formidable supporters of the war, and now their views were ranged against his.

There were also in the background the warnings from Secretary of the Treasury Fowler that another massive troop increase could seriously weaken the dollar in world markets. There was the verbal crossfire from the New Hampshire ambush, where Senator Eugene McCarthy, fighting a presidential primary, was attacking "President Johnson's war"—an attack with a second prong in the form of Senator Robert Kennedy, who by then had also jumped into the electoral fray.

Inside the Administration, Mr. Clifford continued to bear down on the President. He himself was unhappy about making the President's life miserable, but he stood his ground, firmly opposing both troop escalation and continuation of the bombing. Anyone who has ever tried to argue with Mr. Johnson knows what this entailed. It was like suddenly seeing a bulldozer coming at you. One of his former senior advisers now says: "It was never a good idea to tell him directly what you thought. It was difficult to give him direct advice. You had to find methods of communicating with him. My preference was by memo." But Clifford held fast and withstood a lot of punishment.

Contrary to his habit, the President did not try to force a unanimous recommendation. He refused to order a total bombing halt, but he began to lean a little against the request for 206,000 men. Clifford persisted in pleading for at least a partial bombing halt. Why not limit bombing to the Twentieth Parallel? If the U.S. took a first, limited step, perhaps Hanoi would reciprocate. And after a step on both sides, perhaps in the end both might begin walking.

Suddenly, on March 28, the President asked Clifford to put his ideas about a partial halt on paper for possible inclusion in the speech Mr. Johnson was to make on March 31. He wanted to study them; he did not now seem as opposed to the idea of a partial halt as he had been to a total halt. Philip Goulding, the Assistant Secretary for Public Affairs and one of Clifford's closest aides, prepared the draft.

Meanwhile, on March 24, General Wheeler had flown out to the Philippines, at the President's request, to meet General Westmoreland at Clara air base; the purpose was to prepare Westmoreland for what he might expect, since it was already clear from the long-drawn-out consultations in Washington that the President would not agree to call up the reserves. After their meeting, Westmoreland sent word through Wheeler that the earlier uncertainties in Vietnam had largely disappeared, and that no major reinforcements were required.

This was what President Johnson had hoped to be told. Westmoreland said that he wanted to retain troops already received, and would need only combat support and combat service support troops to balance out the brigade of Army paratroopers and the regiments of marines. On March 28 General Westmoreland formally requested an augmentation of 13,500 additional troops and authority to hire additional civilian employees. This request was subsequently approved in its entirety.

On March 28, the same day that Mr. Johnson asked Clifford for his ideas on paper, some of the President's key advisers met in Mr. Rusk's dark-paneled office on the seventh floor of the State Department to put the final touches to the speech the President was to deliver on March 31. Those present, apart from Rusk, were Clifford, Rostow, and William Bundy; Joseph Califano, the President's Administrative Assistant; and Harry McPherson, the President's speech-writer and legal counselor. One of them said afterwards that it was the most important moment of his entire service in the White House.

Before them was a draft—the seventh—which in content reflected the views of Rusk and Rostow. It contained well-worn phrases pleading for peace, but its general thrust was the need for tenacity. It announced that about 15,000 men would be sent as reinforcements to Vietnam, but said nothing about a partial bombing halt.

Clifford, above all, appealed to Rusk that this speech was far too hardboiled and uncompromising. He could not go along with it, he said. He wanted the President to come away from the edge of the precipice where he continually stood, to make clear that he was thinking no longer of escalation but of how to winch down the war. He wanted him to talk peace and to offer at least a partial bombing halt: "I can't be in a position of polishing a speech I disagree with." But the crucial moment came when Clifford asserted that "the Establishment had turned against the war"—meaning the heads of the big industrial corporations and the financial world, the men who make the U.S. tick. It was this final argument that seemed to make the deepest impression on those present.

To everyone's surprise, not even Rusk continued to oppose the idea of a partial halt. None of them knew that in one of his rare and very secret memos to the President, on March 3, 1968, he had himself suggested something along those lines—though on the assumption that the enemy would not respond.

Harry McPherson worked through the night to redraft the speech. When next morning the President queried a passage on the third page of the draft, McPherson found to his great relief that Mr. Johnson was referring to a page in the new text. His stubbornness had given way, and he had accepted Clifford's new approach. For the first time in the war the President had rejected a major request by the military. This was in the long run even more important an event than the speech he was about to make.

Nobody is quite certain why Clifford prevailed. Perhaps it was because the President knew that he was a loyal friend (though over this particular episode, paradoxically, they became estranged), that he had been a hawk, that he had no axe to grind, and that he had brought a fresh mind to the problem. It may have been the grudging recognition that America was dangerously torn, for Clifford had warned the President that an intensification of the war could hold the seeds of the country's destruction. Perhaps it was the simple feeling that the decision was right.

VIII

Through the Maze to Paris

The President began to ease into a less tense mood. The decision had been taken, the agony was almost over. On Saturday, March 30, McPherson put his finishing touches to the speech. The President hinted to him and Clifford that he might have "a speech of his own." McPherson wondered to Clifford: "Do you think he is going to say *sayonara?*"

Next day Horace Busby, a former speech-writer for Mr. Johnson, and George Christian, the President's Press Secretary, worked on the sting in the tail of the speech, which was to be delivered that day, March 31 —the announcement of his withdrawal from the presidential race for the succeeding term.

That morning the President also saw Robert McNamara, whom he had avoided for months, and spent four hours with him going over the speech. McNamara was elated by the decision for a partial bombing halt. In the late spring of 1967 his own aides had drafted a similar proposal, involving the Nineteenth and Twentieth

Parallels, to reverse the process of escalation and to be offered to Hanoi as an inducement to start talks; but its transmission via the Kissinger channel to Hanoi had not been allowed. (Not surprisingly, some, such as McNamara, wonder now whether, had it been allowed to go forward, negotiations might have come to pass earlier.)

When McNamara left the President that Sunday morning, he was both hopeful and exhilarated: "Johnson's mills grind slow"—but they grind. By 4 P.M. Horace Busby had handed in his draft of the abdication declaration.

Secretary Clifford and his wife were invited to the Executive Mansion half an hour before the President was to go on national television. Clifford already knew that he would announce the bombing cutback and the 13,500 more troops. But not until the President motioned him into his bedroom and silently handed him these last two paragraphs of the speech did he know for certain of Mr. Johnson's withdrawal:

> With America's sons in the fields far away, with America's future under challenge right here at home, with our hopes and the world's hopes for peace in the balance every day, I do not believe that I should devote an hour or a day of my time to any personal partisan causes or to any duties other than the awesome duties of this office—the Presidency of your country.
>
> Accordingly, I shall not seek, and I will not accept, the nomination of my party for another term as your President.

The announcement shook the nation and it shook the world. Only a few days earlier, Lyndon B. Johnson's place in history had looked abysmally dim. The country was divided as never since the Civil War, and the abuse heaped on the President was unprecedented in modern times. His surprise abdication had overtones that were both heroic and tragic: it was an admission of failure clothed in an act of statesmanship. Here was a man ruined by the faults, so to speak, of his own virtues. His credibility rating was so low that even his closest friends admitted that they never believed he would refuse another term of office. What they forgot was that though Mr. Johnson was a proud, vain, self-centered, and imperious man, he was also a realist. It had become obvious to him that even if he won the elections, after the savage, internecine fight that they would involve, he would not have the power and influence to heal the wounds, reunite the nation, and prevent political paralysis in Congress.

The nation had scarcely recovered from the upheaval caused by the President's speech when sixty hours later, and to everybody's surprise, Hanoi reacted positively to Mr. Johnson's announcement of a unilateral limited bombing halt without conditions. It was an extraordinarily far-reaching step for the President, for he asked Hanoi to agree to nothing. He tried to make clear that he was prepared to step back by limiting bombing to the Twentieth Parallel and that further steps would depend on whether the enemy would reciprocate in some way.

Through the Maze to Paris

It was, in fact, less an offer to enter into negotiations than an offer for tacit de-escalation or even tacit disengagement. It was Hanoi who interpreted the speech as an offer to negotiate. The first break in the long diplomatic stalemate seemed at hand.

Thirty-six hours afterwards, America's nervous system suffered another severe shock: the Reverend Dr. Martin Luther King, Jr., the apostle of Negro non-violence, was assassinated in Memphis. Even as arrangements for the first serious peaceful exchanges of the Vietnam war were being made, armed airborne troops were being lifted into Washington to help protect the White House and quell the Negro rioting only a few blocks away.

There is some reason to assume that Hanoi had come to much the same conclusion as Washington, and at the same time, about the need for negotiations. Its leaders, too, had realized that they could not win a military victory. Indeed, the alacrity with which they accepted the President's offer led the experts to think that they might have been ready to make some kind of offer themselves. The Tet offensive, after all, had not accomplished what Hanoi had hoped for—the fall of the Saigon Government—and that must have led to a revaluation in the North Vietnamese Politburo.

What seemed to corroborate this assumption was that, unexpectedly, the Hanoi regime had issued a visa to Charles Collingwood, one of the most experienced and respected foreign correspondents of the Columbia Broadcasting System. He had been to South Vietnam several times, and his brilliant reports, though factual, had a hawkish rather than a doveish tinge. No one, therefore, was more surprised than Collingwood that Hanoi should have chosen him at this particular time. From the start it was obvious that he had been selected for special treatment. The appointments he requested with some of North Vietnam's leaders were arranged with unusual speed. Most likely he would have been the man to break the news of the Politburo's change of heart, had President Johnson's offer not overtaken it.

After some acrimonious haggling over the conference site, Paris finally became the obvious compromise, but throughout May and most of June the talks only limped along. The President became unhappy and began to wonder whether he had made another mistake. Some of his aides suggested that he issue an ultimatum, and he came dangerously near to doing so.

In Paris, after several unproductive sessions in public, Ambassador Averell Harriman and his deputy, Cyrus Vance (both men endowed with great patience), decided that in order to find some common ground they would have to go into private session. The first approaches to this end were made in May, but the North Vietnamese were clearly waiting for instructions from Hanoi, and it was not until late in June that the yes was finally passed along. The first private meeting—they occurred at various levels between members of the two delegations—was among the Press officers.

The North Vietnamese were cordial and correct, but it took time before actual negotiations developed. The central problem was to get them to agree to three basic conditions. President Johnson wanted specific assurances about a cessation of attacks against the cities, about halting infiltration across the Demilitarized Zone, and about productive talks which would follow promptly and include the South Vietnamese Government.

Late in July, Harriman and Vance tried to persuade the President to agree to a complete bombing halt. They argued that he could point to the end of the shelling of the cities and a marked decrease in the fighting as an indication that the North was meeting his demands for reciprocal restraints. Clifford had begun to press Mr. Johnson for such a halt even some time earlier, pointing out how each small step, such as restricting the bombing, had changed the climate, and how this course was worth pursuing. Vice-President Humphrey was quite obviously anxious at that point to get the bombing stopped, but some of the President's advisers and Justice Abe Fortas counseled against such a move. The President turned it down.

The longer the sparring in Paris went on without any result, the more the President resented having given in to Clifford's advice. Their relationship became cold and distant, and Clifford's direct telephone line with the President remained silent.

Then, toward the end of September, the North Vietnamese brought the matter up, saying that if the Americans stopped all bombing, they would talk about matters of substance. The crux of the problem in getting down to these matters was how to avoid the word "conditions" for points on which the U.S. was insisting; subsequently the wording became "circumstances which would permit serious talks to go on."

Finally, progress was made when the Russians joined a strange triangular diplomatic minuet. Harriman had said for a long time that the Russians' cooperation was the key to negotiations. He knew them well and they trusted him, believing him when he said that his aim was to advance the cause of peace.

But the Russians had clearly also decided on their own that the time was now propitious for them to assist. Before Harriman left Washington for Paris, he saw the Russian Ambassador, Mr. Dobrynin, with whom he enjoyed about as good a personal relationship as there can be between American and Soviet diplomats. As a result of their meeting, the Russian Ambassador in Paris, Mr. Zorin, was instructed to keep in touch and to facilitate the talks. He first paid a courtesy call on Harriman, and from then on either he, or, in his absence, his Minister, became party to the negotiations. Theirs was a strange, highly sporadic use of the lubricating can; sometimes they were unavailable for weeks and then, suddenly, they were available; sometimes they even took the initiative. The Russians wanted to avoid their own confrontation with the U.S., which might become inevitable if the war simply continued, and they probably were seeking also to gain an important voice in Southeast Asia.

Relations between Hanoi and Peking, meanwhile, had become strained. Russian supplies were being delayed on the Chinese border, and North Vietnamese delegations to the Chinese capital were not being treated as friends and allies. However, when the North Vietnamese were asked about their relations with the Russians or the Chinese, they always replied that they were nationalists, and the less they had to do with either of them the better. Once during one of the private "tea-breaks" in Paris, Mr. Harriman offered them caviar that he had just received from Iran. They declined it, but added that when Mr. Kosygin had offered caviar to the North Vietnamese representatives on a visit to Moscow, they hadn't taken it from him, either.

A curious dialogue of the mute developed. The U.S. asked for confirmation of its conditions for stopping the bombing, and, although no direct answer came forth, indications were nevertheless received that Hanoi was hearing what was being said. Confirmation that they also understood what they were hearing, and were willing to follow through, came haltingly via the Russians. When Hanoi at times procrastinated too much, and the U.S. indicated that it could not continue the bombing halt without some indication that the halt was worthwhile, word came back from the Russians that it was.

By October 11, thanks to Harriman's skill in dealing with Communists and his shrewd way of being able to roll with the punches of this delicate, diplomatic shadow-boxing, a point had been reached at which the North Vietnamese indicated (again through the Russians) what amounted to acceptance of the American conditions. A bombing halt now appeared to be a real possibility—and at this stage could have had a major effect on the presidential election campaign. But then the White House instructed Harriman to demand that peace talks must follow within twenty-four hours of the halt. Only if a meeting took place almost immediately, the President felt, could he avoid being accused of playing election politics. He had told Mr. Nixon what his terms were and he was going to stand by his words.

The North Vietnamese resisted. They wanted more time, up to two weeks, to elapse before talks, to obscure the fact that they now agreed to conditional negotiations after insisting for years that they would never do so. In addition, they were put out by rumors of a "breakthrough" in Paris that emanated from the presidential palace in Saigon. (These rumors implied that Hanoi had agreed to the American conditions. President Thieu had been informed of Hanoi's position on October 15, and he seemed ready to go along, though at that point he had had no opportunity to place the matter before a wider circle of his entourage.) In what looked like an angry countermove, Hanoi suddenly demanded a written agreement, which they said would not be for publication, that the bombing halt was "unconditional." They also wanted spelled out who would participate in the negotiations, and they demanded a longer interval between the end of the bombing and the start of the talks. But when Ambassador Harriman made it absolutely clear that President Johnson could not sign such a statement, they withdew the demand altogether.

There is little doubt that the North Vietnamese were, in the end, anxious to bring about an agreement, and that one of the main reasons for their hurry was to influence the American elections. They did not want Mr. Nixon to win. They had read reports of his implied threat, made during the Republican Convention in Miami, to use nuclear weapons in Vietnam, and they didn't like it. They preferred Hubert Humphrey. They were now even willing to sit down with the Saigon Government, which they used to call "imperialist puppet."

When the word was flashed from Paris on October 27 that the deal was clinched, President Johnson called his Vietnam commander, General Abrams, back to Washington. On October 11, when the North Vietnamese had indicated for the first time that they would accept the American conditions, Abrams and Ambassador Bunker in Saigon had agreed that "this is the time to move" and that it would be sensible for the President to go along.

After a long, tiring flight, Abrams arrived in the Cabinet Room of the White House at 2:30 A.M. on October 29. No one asked him, in the normal courteous way, what sort of a flight he had had. All those assembled somehow felt that everybody was in the front line, that the Cabinet Room too was part of it. The President immediately explained to Abrams that the North Vietnamese had accepted all his conditions. Looking at the whole situation, he would have to order the end of the bombing, but did not want to issue the order "before he had looked him in the eye." Then he added: "We got them to Paris not by the cleverness of diplomacy, but by your go-go."

Abrams looked solid and composed. "I don't know all the pressures on the Presidency," his reply began firmly, "and I cannot assess all the dimensions, but I know we have to make a contribution to the new environment. I know that you are plunged into a cesspool of different motives at different times, but I believe that it is right to go ahead because to stop the bombing would get the talks off dead center and I believe the war ought to be ended at the conference table." He looked the President straight in the eye and suddenly, as one participant put it, it became clear why the President had replaced General Westmoreland with General Abrams.

There was a price, though, that the military extracted from the President for their acceptance of the end of the bombing of North Vietnam. They insisted that they must be allowed to exert "maximum pressure" on the enemy in the South. This was agreed. In the following month, according to Ambassador Harriman, this produced conflicting results: some of the regular North Vietnamese units that had withdrawn across the Demilitarized Zone or into Laos or Cambodia returned to South Vietnam. But no one can say for certain whether their reentry was generated by the American strategy of "maximum pressure" or whether they had merely withdrawn temporarily to be reequipped.

The negotiations logjam seemed broken. Then suddenly the "imperialist puppet" balked. President Thieu reneged on his acceptance of the Paris agreement, to Ambassador Bunker's great embarrassment. It infuriated Washington, for the talks about talks had been dragging on for nearly six weeks, and now, when at last Hanoi had agreed to admit the "imperialist puppet" to the conference table, and the final obstacle had been removed, Saigon dragged her feet. What was the President to do? Should he delay a deal because his ally was trying to obstruct it, or should he proceed without him? He decided that a solid commitment that included firm dates was a commitment whether it was to an ally or a foe, and so he told Thieu that he would announce the end of the bombing that night (October 31), and it would actually stop next morning. The President's advisers were unanimous in telling him that he had to proceed; he could not afford to be put in a position where it might "leak" to the public that he and Thieu had reneged on an agreement that he had put to Hanoi.

Lurking behind Thieu's calculated delays, American

intelligence sources established, was a powerful attempt —worthy of the imagination of Ian Fleming—by some Nixon backers (including two Republican senators) to hold up the announcement of the bombing halt until after the American elections. Allegedly, Mrs. Anna Chennault, the Chinese widow of the famous founder of the Flying Tigers—who is well-connected in Formosa and Saigon, and is an ardent Republican—provided the "good offices." The argument as put to Thieu ran something like this: "Don't let the Democrats force you into a deal that will put Humphrey in the White House—he'll be worse for you than Nixon." No evidence was found that Mr. Nixon himself had any inkling of this bizarre conspiracy.

Nobody will ever be able to prove that the delay cost Hubert Humphrey and the Democratic Party the election. But if the Nixon men are correct in assuming that much of Humphrey's last-minute upsurge among voters was due to the announcement of the halt six days before election day, then it is possible to speculate that an earlier announcement might have lifted Humphrey to a narrow victory.

Clark Clifford's individual battles, meanwhile, were by no means over. His indignation came to the boil when Saigon first claimed that they had to call their ambassador back to Washington for consultations before they could send a delegation to the Paris talks, and

then that the decision had to be presented to their legis-
lative assembly—all excuses for delay. Fearing that
Saigon was trying to torpedo the talks, Clifford decided
to go on what some called a "crusade."

Five days after the election, Clifford said publicly that
"the President had the responsibility to proceed with
the agreement, because getting on with the talks, which
could end the war, far transcended in importance whatever some political result might be." He created opportunities at press conferences to talk to Saigon over
the heads of his colleagues in the Administration, he
gave interviews on television and made speeches—all
this without either approval or disapproval from the
President.

His actions brought to a head the disagreement between, on the one hand, Clifford, who did not believe
in perpetuating the Thieu regime, and, on the other,
Rusk, Rostow, and Bunker, who regarded such an idea
as close to treason; the disagreement became a fierce and
fundamental conflict. Clifford argued for stronger pressure to be applied on Saigon; for too long, he thought,
Saigon had been able to exercise a veto over American
decisions. He doubted that the South Vietnamese had
any desire to negotiate, or any real willingness to assume responsibility for their own defense. They neither
wanted the U.S. to withdraw her troops, which represented their best police force, nor to see a reduction in
the enormous injection of U.S. financial aid. Their goal,

Clifford thought, was to keep Americans fighting indefinitely—and something had to be done to disabuse them of *that* idea.

President Johnson, though, failed to react to Clifford's proddings on the need to speak more bluntly to Thieu. Instead, Clifford's passionate impatience was countered by his opponents with the argument that the Saigon Government had more political strength than any of its predecessors, that it had its own elected Constitutional Assembly, and had built up its army into a serious fighting force. To succumb to Clifford's arguments, they insisted, could undermine it and endanger everything that the U.S. had achieved at such great cost.

President Thieu did not quite succeed in delaying the negotiations until President Nixon was installed in the White House. He finally sent his envoy, General Ky, to Paris on December 2, but negotiations of substance began only on January 8—too late to preserve whatever momentum Harriman and Vance had created. But the fact that the government of Saigon and representatives of the National Liberation Front were now facing each other across the conference table was living proof that the conflict on the battlefield had been played to a bloody draw.

IX

Epilogue:
The Ultimate Verdict

In a curious way ideology and rationalism, rare bed-fellows, made common cause in dragging the United States into the morass of Vietnam. The ideology, born in the cold war, gave the initial momentum. It led President Truman and President Eisenhower to provide the aid and also the rhetoric needed to obtain Congressional and public support. The rhetoric was based primarily on the fear that having lost China to Communism, the U.S. would also lose the rest of Asia. Later the fears of another "Munich," of another Korea, and of the Democrats being accused of "softness" on Communism helped to reinforce the rhetoric and the reasoning.

The rationalism was added later, and was born of the Cuban missile crisis. That brilliant success in averting thermonuclear war by the application of the coolest of cool rationalism—the "graduated response"—provided one of the new wisdoms of the nuclear age. President Kennedy, after weighing all the odds and "trying to understand the implications of every move," rejected the direct and immediate use of force. He decided in favor of a slow crescendo of military measures that avoided direct confrontation and immediate retaliation, but clearly pointed at the possible and likely consequences if the graduated response was allowed to reach its climax.

It was the product of calm, steady, almost nerveless thinking, and of the coolest possible assessment of the enemy's intentions. John Kennedy, his brother Robert, McGeorge Bundy, and Robert McNamara were the architects of this flexible strategy and the true believers in the intellectual process and its rational products. Robert Kennedy's history of the Cuban missile crisis is the textbook to the graduated response, and convincingly proves its validity. It therefore became the answer to containing the risks of direct nuclear confrontation that threaten every time a superpower is involved in war or a warlike situation. It succeeded in Cuba against the Soviet Union: logic suggested that it ought also to be effective—or more so, since it had to deal with actual conflict—against a small country such as North Vietnam. The graduated response therefore became a major influence on American military strategy in the Johnson phase of the war.

For President Kennedy, Vietnam remained a sideshow. The risks of half-baked action were not high then, and he was constantly buying more time, first with President Diem, then without him. Equally, the domestic political risks did not seem high at the time, and therefore he had no compelling need to disengage. Kennedy mounted the tiger, but it was Johnson's lot to choose the difficult moment for jumping off.

When President Johnson took over, he was at first trapped by his slogan, "Let us continue": it soon became, "We are not going to be defeated." The theory of the need to "contain" Communism in Asia as enunciated by Truman was basic to Johnson's thinking; and his determination "not to be the first American President to lose a war" was basic to his character.

The Eisenhower theory of "massive retaliation" offered no solution in Vietnam. It was accepted doctrine in the U.S. Government that if North Vietnam were, as the Air Force General Curtis LeMay suggested, "bombed into the Stone Age," China would not allow a vacuum to develop and would move into Vietnam as she did into Korea. Such a strategy was also morally unacceptable.

McNamara, therefore, in a dazzling intellectual display, revamped the American military machine and provided it with the weapons, equipment, and training to fight limited wars with the "graduated response." The U.S. first warned the enemy by bombing North Vietnam, then threatened bigger and bigger—open-ended —troop commitments. The rationalists expected that they could frighten Hanoi to the conference table.

The ideologists mistrusted the "graduated response": they favored quick escalation, and they were committed to victory. They did not believe that a worthwhile settlement could be reached by talking. The principal ideologists were Dean Rusk and Walt W. Rostow. Both were obsessed by the war and the need to win it at almost any cost short of the use of nuclear weapons. They were skeptical of bombing pauses and peace feelers, which they saw as signs of weakness. They believed in rapid and concentrated application of power and, if necessary, the hard slog to victory. Both profoundly resented the fact that the U.S. had to fight in Vietnam, unlike in Korea, without major allies. The British Government's refusal to send even a token force angered them both, and led to many heated and futile arguments between Washington and London. What both liked to overlook was that there existed a formal agreement that Britain would not ask the U.S. to contribute troops to the defense of Borneo in the "confrontation" with Sukarno's Indonesia, and the U.S. in turn would not demand that British troops be sent to fight along with the Americans in Vietnam.

Such doves as George Ball (who was the most persistent) and perhaps also Llewellyn Thompson, the United States Ambassador to the Soviet Union, did not think that the American involvement in Vietnam made either political or military sense. They believed in Europe's being the key to American interests.

President Johnson was certain for a long time that bombing would bring results. He believed that by watching every target hit by the Air Force he could make it a sanitized war. "If they hit people," he used to say, "I'll bust their asses." Limited war became his worst dilemma. It was against his nature, against the nature of the military; in effect, it was against the nature of war itself. As one of Mr. Johnson's aides once put it: "It was like stimulating a woman close to ecstasy and then leaving her with only a chaste kiss on the cheek."

One of Johnson's great handicaps was his inability to rally the country. Another was that he had to conduct the first war brought live and "in living color" via television into every American home. Never before have the horrors of war been exposed to those living safely in the far-away rear, in those cities and farmlands on the American continent that have never experienced destruction from air raids or rockets.

One of Johnson's great weaknesses was that he had in mind no clearly defined objectives. He thought he had, but—as one of his friends, whom he often consulted, puts it—"They were all words. He is a man who verbalizes everything and who thought that words which he changed from time to time amounted to clear objectives. He did not really understand the full impact of the war on America, he thought he could disregard it. Nor did he understand the danger any President is exposed to, of being isolated from a broad range of information."

Johnson firmly believed in fighting the war to the end, because he was convinced that in the end the mili-

tary situation just had to get better; and he was, anyway, constantly told that there were growing indications
that the U.S. was doing better, always a little better.
He had a desperate need to believe that that was so.
War was not an obsession with him—far from it—but
victory was.

What really changed his mind in the days preceding
his "abdication" speech of March 31, 1968, is one of the
most intriguing, most puzzling missing links in the affair. In that great inner drama the Polonius, the Clau-
dius, the Horatio, the Laertes, the others all were there,
all played their parts; but the Prince of Denmark is
missing, and no one is certain who or where or what he
was. There is no doubt among his closest aides that if
the speech had been made on March 20, it would have
been a speech of Churchillian blood and thunder. Instead he reached out for peace.

Was this because of his abdication decision? More
probably it was due to a confluence of circumstances:
the great influence of Clark Clifford, Dean Acheson,
and a few others, the pleadings of Mrs. Johnson (who
thought that he would not survive another four years
in the White House), a family poll around Christmas-
time that showed virtually his entire family in favor of
his retirement (including one of his sons-in-law who
had served in Vietnam), and the prospect of confronta-
tions with Senator Eugene McCarthy and (especially)
Senator Robert Kennedy. As Ray Scherer, of the National Broadcasting Company, an old hand at analyzing

presidential minds, wrote to me: "He quit, so to speak, while he was behind."

President Johnson was often torn between his desire for peace and for military victory, and with victory seemingly remote, it may have been more appetizing in the end to seek to step back into history with the bells of peace ringing. Will he ever reveal the truth? Perhaps when he comes to write about those days he will justify the change of heart by trying to prove that there was no change at all. Clark Clifford is honest enough to admit that if he had become Secretary of Defense earlier, he would probably have acted as his predecessors did, but in 1968 circumstances made it easier to reach the conclusions he came to, and to see the need for the ship of state to change course.

Robert McNamara forfeited the President's confidence and was eased out earlier than he expected because he had lost faith in the prosecution and the purpose of the war. He thought for a long time that an attempt had to be made to win the war, and thought also that there was a way to do it. He had always assumed that if you put your shoulder to the wheel, you could accomplish anything; this was basic to his philosophy of life. But by the middle of 1966, he had come to realize that the political and human costs in Vietnam were too high. He had become a disturbing influence on the President, because Johnson, in his own mind, was committed to winning the war. While McNamara disturbed him, George Ball was tolerated, but only because the President liked the idea of his arguing the case for the other side; he was rarely persuaded, but he was willing to listen to Ball.

The failure of the graduated response came to haunt McNamara. He and others like McGeorge Bundy were convinced that if you approach people rationally, it will lead to a rational solution. They assumed that they were dealing with rational people, who after being hurt and frightened would come to the conference table. But war ceased to be a rational instrument. When the enemy failed to operate by rational rules, the situation became increasingly perplexing. It also became increasingly obvious that the U.S. did not know enough about the nature of the enemy, about his inner strength and endurance. In addition, the rational expectations of air power were highly exaggerated.

There was another serious flaw in applying to Vietnam the theory that succeeded so well in Cuba. Not enough credit had been given to the distance between the Soviet Union and Cuba. It must have been evident to the Russians that they could not exercise remote control over the situation; that may in fact have been one of the principal reasons for their decision to withdraw the missiles. When the U.S. began to apply the graduated-response technique to Vietnam, it did not pay enough regard to the distance of that country from the American shores or to the fact that it was geographically so close to both Russia and China. Both these factors made it infinitely more difficult to control both the military and the political situations in Vietnam. These were two of the rocks on which rational thought foundered.

Senator William Fulbright, Chairman of the Senate Foreign Relations Committee, and Senator Eugene McCarthy, the presidential aspirant, were wrong in maintaining that there was an honorable, cheap way of getting out of Vietnam without its going Communist. No such option existed. To take that fork in the road always implied a high probability of a Communist takeover. The choice was always, from the very beginning, between a bad and an uncertain outcome. There was usually complete agreement that withdrawal would be bad. But there was disagreement whether fighting on was worse or better than withdrawing. No one gave enough thought to whether it was all worthwhile. No one predicted what a prolonged war in Vietnam would do to American society.

Very few people, and this includes Americans, are aware that the U.S. Government has no secure way of ensuring that a military strategy chosen by the military command fits in with the Administration's political objectives. President Johnson carefully supervised the Air Force's bombing targets and so did McNamara, but neither interfered with the military strategy in the field, which was based on the simple directive to exert "maximum military pressure on the enemy." This would, it was assumed, force the enemy into a political settlement. How this pressure was to be exerted was left to the military. The accepted rule is that everybody must trust the judgment of the commander in the field; not even the Joint Chiefs of Staff are supposed to interfere.

I remember asking McNamara once during an interview in late 1967 whether he ever tried to influence military strategy in the field, for it seemed to me then, after my visit to Vietnam, that the "search and destroy" strategy could be made less costly. But he said firmly that he did not try to intervene, because he did not understand enough about military strategy; this had to be left to the men on the spot. I made the point that Winston Churchill had been a civilian leader who often influenced military strategy, admittedly not always beneficially, but McNamara insisted that (a) he was no Churchill, and (b) he did not want to go against the rule in this particular area of competence. The only way he could have intervened drastically was by cutting down the number of fighting men in Vietnam. It was in fact just such a drastic action—the President's decision against sending 206,000 additional men—that compelled a change, if not in strategy, then in political aim. What became known only later was that whatever the political aim (1965–1967, to achieve military victory; 1967–1968, to settle for a compromise through negotiations with the enemy; or, as from March 31, 1968, when negotiations to end the war were already in progress), the military strategy remained the same.

Unless, therefore, the President himself feels confident enough to change military strategy, there is no one who dares to interfere with the military's own judgment, and no machinery through which control can be exercised. Nor has the Vietnam experience led to the development of a mechanism that would ensure coordination between the Government's political objectives and those of the military commanders in the field.

The United Nations, for its part, only exposed its impotence. The U.S. did not want to make too much use of it, because the United States did not want to force the Soviet Union into irretrievable opposition and because, at best, it could only serve as a propaganda forum. The North Vietnamese resented the U.N., as they were not members. And Secretary-General U Thant lost whatever influence he might have been able to exert as a go-between because he was considered in Washington as having a strong bias in favor of Hanoi. There is little doubt that the so-called "peace feelers" were often carelessly handled. Perhaps Hanoi would simply not have entered into negotiations until, in April, 1968, both sides recognized that the war had reached a stalemate; and many feelers were obviously self-serving or mistimed or even dishonest. But because of the carelessness, uneasy doubts remain about whether in a few cases real opportunities were missed.

The war is still going on and men are being killed. It is still the enemy, not the Americans, who control the level of American casualties. "Death became the official measure of success," as James Reston put it, but it proved to be a deceptive one.

In the peace talks the North Vietnamese have several advantages. They know that the United States is not willing to continue the war indefinitely. It is the cost, not so much the basic principle or the morality, that has come to disturb Americans. Hanoi has almost unlimited manpower and can assume that sooner, rather than later, it will be able to control or at least exert an influence in South Vietnam. But it has lost a whole generation of young men. The North is ravaged by the war, and social progress has been delayed for many years. No nation can afford such conditions indefinitely. And as in all wars that end in a stalemate, neither side finds it easy to compromise; both want to make certain that their sacrifices were not in vain.

Those who played an important role in U.S. policy-making can be divided roughly into four groups according to their retrospective assessment of the war. There are those, like Rusk and Rostow, who are unhappy that the U.S. acceded to negotiations at a time when she could not bargain from strength. They remain convinced that the opposition at home was containable and that there is no real alternative to victory. They maintain that the U.S. was on the way toward victory, and that events will confirm their profound skepticism about the talks.

There are those who favor negotiations and de-escalation of the war but who also believe that, as McGeorge Bundy put it, "When the history of these years—of this whole generation—comes to be written, it will be clear that in these two years a hard corner was turned in a way which will have the same meaning in its fashion for the future of South Asia and the Western Pacific that the defense of Korea had further north, the defense of Berlin had for Europe, and the Cuban missile crisis had for all . . ." His brother William, who stayed the course as Assistant Secretary for Far Eastern Affairs, shares this view.

There are those, and Robert McNamara is probably one of them, who have come to doubt the wisdom of American involvement in Vietnam because of the enormous disparity between the costs and the gains, and because of what the war has done to the fabric of American society and to the American outlook on the world.

And finally there are those, such as George Ball and Paul Nitze, who continue to feel what they have felt from the start, that the war was a big mistake.

Some, especially in Congress, are worried that without final victory the Air Force and American military prestige in general will have suffered. But the American nuclear deterrent remains inviolate, and the military can claim either that the restraints imposed on them made victory impossible, or that they were on the road to victory but deprived of it by the decision to go to the conference table. In fact, the prestige of the military suffered only because their assessments of the war situation proved wrong too often. That was General West-moreland's curse, but perhaps even more so that of his predecessors.

The American military command must accept the blame for having taken too long to adjust its tactics to guerrilla warfare—if it ever really succeeded in doing so. It continued to believe in the application of over-whelming power, which disintegrated like a high-explo-sive bomb in desert sand. It based its strategy on win-ning the war with American troops, and neglected for too long the training and equipping of the South Viet-namese forces. It used a far too inflexible strategy, and it refused to take into consideration that the higher the casualties, the more likely the war was to lose support at home. In a war when both sides "fight for time, not space," as C. L. Sulzberger of the *New York Times* wrote, "the most important objectives are distant from the battlefield."

The U.S., thanks to a fine fighting force and over-whelming resources, turned defeat into a draw and staved off the takeover of South Vietnam by Hanoi. It has clothed the Saigon regime with legitimacy, as that government's acceptance by North Vietnam and by the National Liberation Front at the Paris talks testifies. But America has been forced to put its hopes of peaceful political change in Saigon at the mercy of NLF partici-pation in free elections. Whether these elections will lead to a government that can maintain its independ-ence and neutrality, whether in fact there ever will be elections, is doubtful; whether this still matters in a world where nationalism is interfering with Communist unity is also doubtful. But in this lies the ultimate test of U.S. intervention, and the ultimate verdict of American public opinion.

The war has deeply divided the nation, brought out many latent domestic problems, and revived and accentuated an always latent isolationism. Premier Kosygin has proved the point he made in an interview with *Life* magazine when he said: "We, for our part, will do all we can so that the United States does not defeat Vietnam."

As for the U.S., one can say with Baudelaire that the war has brought home to Americans that the U.S. is no more *"consciente et reine d'elle-même"*—she is no longer mistress of herself.

INDEX

Index

Index

Laos, 4, 20, 151; American interest in, 11, 14–17
LeMay, General Curtis, 157
Lewandowski, Janusz, 73–77, 79
Lippmann, Walter, 53
Lodge, Henry Cabot, 25, 73, 74–77, 79, 81, 132; his ten-point peace proposal, 75–77; Kissinger's mission for, 103
London *Sunday Times*, 10, 113

McCarthy, Eugene, 135, 160, 163
McClellan, George (Civil War general), 119
McCloy, John, 132
McGiffert, David E., 128
Macmillan, Harold, 15
McNamara, Robert, 3, 21, 22–23, 29, 30, 37, 41, 167; speech of before Armed Services Committee, 31–32; on military pressure, 52–53; flies to Saigon, 56; and bombing pause, 62; on infiltration, 68; reflects doubts about war, 69; estrangement from Johnson, 71, 140–141, 161; and Wilson-Kosygin talks, 89; and mining of Haiphong Harbor, 102; on Warnke's peace formula, 106; succeeded by Clifford, 109, 121; and bombing of North, 110–112; appointed Director of World Bank, 115; and 1965 bombing

pause, 122–123; and graduated response, 156, 157, 162; and bombing targets, 163–164
McNaughton, John, 47, 67–68, 78
McPherson, Harry, 137, 138, 140
Maddox, U.S. destroyer, 32–33
Malaya, 24
Malaysia, 37
Manila Declaration, 114
Marcovich, Herbert, 103, 104
"Marigold" (peace feeler, 1966), 73–81, 83
Mekong Delta, 19
Mekong River, 53
Michalowski, J., 64, 74, 77
Military Advisory Command Vietnam (MACV), 124, 125
Minh, Major General Duong Van, 31
Minh, Ho Chi, *see* Ho Chi Minh
Moyers, Bill, 40, 62; and policy-making job, 66–67
Munich, 37, 155
Murphy, Robert, 132, 134
Murray, Donald, 87

National Liberation Front (NLF), 55, 61–62, 68, 154, 168
National Security Council, 15, 24, 51
New York Times, 108, 121, 125
New Zealand, 122
Nhan Dang, 64

Index

DATE DUE